BLOOD DYNAMICS

BLOOD DYNAMICS

Anita Y. Wonder

ACADEMIC PRESS

A Harcourt Science and Technology Company

San Diego   San Francisco   New York   Boston
London   Sydney   Tokyo

ACADEMIC PRESS
A Harcourt Science and Technology Company
Harcourt Place, 32 Jamestown Road, London NW1 7BY, UK
http://www.academicpress.com

ACADEMIC PRESS
A Harcourt Science and Technology Company
525 B Street, Suite 1900, San Diego, California 92101-4495, USA
http://www.academicpress.com

ISBN 0-12-762457-0

Library of Congress Control Number 2001089407
A catalogue record for this book is available from the British Library

Typeset by Kenneth Burnley, Wirral, Cheshire
Printed in Spain by Grafos SA Arte Sobre Papel, Barcelona
01 02 03 04 05 06 GF 9 8 7 6 5 4 3 2 1

CONTENTS

ACKNOWLEDGEMENTS

This book has been 14 years in the making. During those years many individuals have contributed to the knowledge, technical and practical, that has gone into it. 'Write the D— Book' became a mantra among close friends. It is impossible to name all to whom I feel a debt, but some special notes are in order. First and foremost is G. Michele Yezzo, of Ohio's BCI&I Lab, as my partner, co-lecturer, interpreter and little sister, she has always been there for me. My appreciation to those who helped find information, sometimes at short notice, goes to Michele as well as Warren Day, John Thornton and Adrian Emes. For my literary search I owe much to my college advisor, Brian Parker. It was with pleasure I discovered Paul Kirk held Brian in great esteem for his professionalism and research techniques. The motto I learned from Brian is 'believe nothing, look it up yourself'. For the interest in clarifying science principles in bloodstain pattern evidence, I credit to Bart Epstein and Terry Laber of Minnesota.

I wouldn't have had so much fun and benefited from all the workshops were it not for the Bloody Workshop crews: Harry Holmes and Dan Watson (with Holmes and Watson for assistants how could we go wrong?), the regulars Dennis Dolezal, JoEllen Latham, and Dean Reichenberg, and in no particular order Captain/Chief of Police Jack Bayer, Sheriff Ken Blake (deceased), Don Tapper, Mary Koompin-Williams, Del Steward, Harvey Gould, Marya Krogstad, John Hughes, and Angela Gallup. Of course those classes, amongst others, were well coordinated by my e-mail funny buddy, Karl B. Hutchinson. My parents, both now gone, supported my quest for information regarding blood behavior in criminal events. I thank my supervisors and managers at the hospital, who helped me juggle my schedule and deal with the stress and strain of producing the final product: Maria Salomon, Mary Combs, and Ron Caretti. Last but definitely not least, I am grateful to my thoughtful and patient editor, Nick Fallon of Academic Press.

For any of you who can visit San Francisco and would like to experience the legacy of Paul Leland Kirk, I recommend that you review his papers at the Bancroft Library. Plan to spend a day or two as there are seven boxes of them, and viewing must be done on site. They provide a personal view of the development for modern forensic science which one experiences while reading it all.

There is a rumor that Paul wrote in code. As John Thornton pointed out, that was not the case. Unfortunately Dr Kirk's handwriting is so illegible it amounts to the same thing, even for one experienced with physicians' handwriting. Nevertheless, there is more than enough clear and concise material to fascinate students of criminalistics and forensic sciences well into the millennium.

ANITA Y. WONDER
February 2001

To

John Patty
(1952–1991)

another great loss to forensic science

Paul Kirk (1902–1970)

CHAPTER 1

INTRODUCTION TO BLOOD DYNAMICS

BACKGROUND

The subject of:

- Blood dynamics[a]
- Bloodstain pattern analysis[b]
- Blood splash[c]
- Blood distribution[d]
- Bloodstain interpretation[e]
- Bloodspatter evidence[f]
- Blood splatters[g]
- Blood spots, spreckles, spray expertise[h]
- Bloodstain dynamics[i]

is as varied as the list of names by which it is known. This publication uses Blood Dynamics in honor of Paul Leland Kirk, PhD (1902–1970). Dr Kirk coined the term for testimony and lectures as a modern science approach to bloodstain patterns. Recognition is given throughout this book for his pioneering contributions to the discipline of Blood Dynamics.

Often the whole discipline is referred to as bloodspatter evidence. The subject actually includes several divisions within the body of information.

DIVISIONS OF BLOOD DYNAMICS

- Evidence recording and collection
- Identification of patterns
- Interpretation and reconstruction of criminal events
- Reconstruction experimentation design
- Adjudication in criminal and civil cases
- Academic research

A common criticism is that the whole field is subjective.[j] In practice all stages can be, although not always are, applied objectively. Casework interpretation and court handling, however, may tempt subjective use. How the evidence will be applied depends on effective training which encourages appreciation for limitations and applicable science principles. Dr Kirk warned attorneys in a

[a] Paul LeLand Kirk title of expertise in the case of People v. Carter, 312 P2nd 665 (1957).

[b] Official title for the discipline accepted by the International Association of Bloodstain Pattern Analyst (IABPA), November 18, 1983.

[c] Term used to describe the evidence in Australia.

[d] Label used in training in the United Kingdom, and found in papers by Dr Kirk.

[e] Court testimony label of expertise Farris v. the State of Oklahoma, 670 P2d 995 (1983).

[f] Popular term such as found in a column on Training and Resources Video, 1999 Second Quarter CAC News, p. 15.

[g] Term not used by most experts on the subject but often encountered in court transcripts, the popular press, and some reports.

[h] Various terms used by attorneys when contacting the author for expertise in the evidence.

[i] Label given international workshops since 1985 presented by the author.

[j] Comments written to the author following a CAC Dinner Meeting on a case application of bloodstain-patterns, 1993.

[k]Dr Kirk often published similar papers to his presentations. The presentation notes were found in the Bancroft Archives at the University of California, Berkeley. Where possible the published work is also listed in the references.

speech, delivered before the 1962 California Trial Lawyers'[k] Association Meeting in San Francisco, regarding the need for interpretation during testimony.[1, 2] He stated that oversimplification can result in 'half truths and even be misleading' to the *trier of fact*. This observation is still pertinent. Objective formats are necessary for bloodstain pattern identification and interpretation.

UNRECORDED HISTORY

Unfortunately for recorded modern history, information regarding blood substance has developed at an overwhelming rate in an increasing variety of science disciplines, such that adequate literature review was not feasible during Dr Kirk's life. With the availability of internet search engines and automated cross references an entirely new perspective is now available. To find this information, however, one must go beyond forensic sciences and historical law enforcement literature.

The field of Blood Dynamics is unique in development. Most forensic disciplines follow discoveries in other sciences. For example, DNA was defined in genetics[3] and applied to biology years before it was tested in crime investigation.[4] By contrast, bloodstain patterns only merit interest within a forensic context. No records show exactly how or when pattern use began in antiquity. Quotes from the Bible symbolically equate bloodstains with injury and mortality.[l] This indicates that blood significance was commonly understood well over 2000 years ago. Indications from paleolithic art history,[5] 4000 years prior to the Bible, suggest that early humans were skilled hunters. The ability to interpret patterns would develop with tracking trades, and be a financial enhancement. Trades people have traditionally trained apprentices with shared stories of experiences. This same approach may be encountered today. An appearance of trade secret legacy may contribute to the subjective label by members of the scientific community.

[l]Genesis 37:31–33.

Other sciences have likely evolved from hunter-tracker origins as well, such as astronomy and geology. The difference in the direction of development for them compared with Blood Dynamics is that applications were found, such as a need for minerals, fossil fuels, space travel, and global communication, which rewarded pure and applied science research. Bloodstain patterns, as the aftermath of injury, are only of concern to law enforcement, a field usually included in the social sciences. Further, industrial sponsors prefer to fund chemical and instrumental projects. This is understandable since those discoveries could enhance sales. Although photography, computer models, and measuring and recording devices can be applied, skills in none of these are required to qualify as an expert in bloodstain pattern evidence.

The lack of funding has led predominantly to a casework research approach.

There are several problems with this, the most obvious being bias. Certain conclusions are desired from the perspective of a specific case which may influence experimental design even by the most open-minded investigator. Time, funding, and biological hazards constraints may produce experiments not substantially similar to the crime alleged. Further, within an individual investigation there may be a variety of participants analyzing information from specialist viewpoints: police identification, general criminalists, trace evidence experts, serologists, DNA examiners, pathologists, detectives, attorneys, and photojournalists. Although efforts have been made to standardize training, terminology, and application for all,[m] attitudes that training be tailored for peer groups are ingrained.[n] Communication between different agencies, even within the same geological area, is often inadequate.

Variance in viewpoints leads to different pattern emphasis. Detectives focus on *spatters*, blood spots, while identification technicians may concentrate on *transfers*, contact patterns such as fingerprints. *Arterial damage* patterns are considered the realm of pathologists. If one individual becomes the in-house expert, his/her perspective may dominate the investigative approach. Bloodstain pattern evidence benefits much more from teamwork concepts, than from a 'super sleuth' approach.

OBJECTIVES

The objectives of this publication are:

- To provide a reference for all pattern types in one source.
- To outline a science-based objective approach to pattern identification.
- To update blood dynamics with technical discoveries from other sciences.

An objective approach is described for identification based on predictable and reproducible criteria. This format has a basis in Paul Kirk's lectures, and has proven beneficial in casework around the world. References are provided from colloid chemistry, fluid mechanics, rheology, biorheology, hematology, and other divisions of science and technology. While the information may appear complex and technical, it need not invalidate competent and conscientious prior casework. The information provided here must, however, be taken into consideration for future research and education to confirm Blood Dynamics as a fully qualified science discipline.

No formal terminology list is provided in this work. Terms are described within the text for understanding of the tools and concepts of the patterns discussed. None of the terms used are to be taken as written in stone. Science, unlike law, is seldom preoccupied with memorizing definitions and semantics.

[m]Bylaws of the International Association of Bloodstain Pattern Analysts, established November 1983 in Corning, New York.

[n]Class comments reviewed by the author following lectures in Death Investigation and Bloodstain Dynamics Workshops.

Terms change as new discoveries and understanding become available. At any given time different levels of the lexicon can be encountered while a science discipline is developing. It is hoped that the information provided will be reviewed for possible application in updating future terminology lists.

Figure 1.1

A microscopic view of a stained blood film.

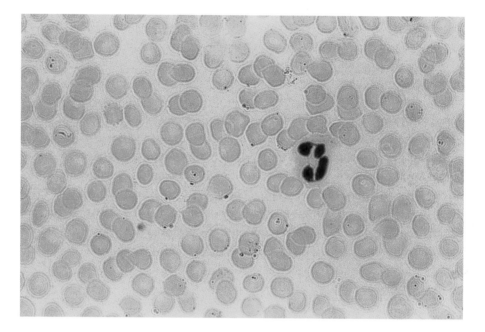

WHAT IS BLOOD?

Blood is not only a complex substance, it is unique. The components of blood have been isolated and synthesized[6] yet nothing presently available performs as satisfactorily in maintaining life. Because blood is so essential, it is always significant at crime scenes. This perhaps explains why experienced law enforcement personnel, even those who lack an academic science background, show a consistent ability to identify blood at crime scenes. This is not to say all are always right. Confirmation is always recommended. Experience, however, has shown that stains viewed as blood by experienced investigators are usually verified with further testing. If nonscientists are able to recognize the substance of blood with regularity, science principles exist to explain that precision. Technical literature confirms that bloodstain patterns are based in scientific principles beyond simple physics.

COMPOSITION

Blood, shown as a microscopic view in Figure 1.1, is a liquid with some dissolved substances, some suspended biological cells and particles,[7] some sedimenting biological cells and particles, some filterable material, and some nonfilterable material. Chemically that makes it a colloid,[8] a true solution, not a true solution, a compound biochemical, and probably many more classifications not listed here.[9] Not all properties of blood concern forensic science application. An illustration of a blood smear is shown in Figure 1.1 with a predominance of red blood cells with one white blood cell.

For bloodstain patterns, two components are important: the liquid, *plasma*, and the major particulate fraction, *red blood cells* (erythrocytes). These are expressed as a percentage of the *packed [red] cell volume* (PCV), also commonly referred to as the *hematocrit*. Figure 1.2 shows capillary measurements for different hematocrits. The hematocrit in humans is not only variable between individuals[10] but also for changes in conditions of a single[11] blood donor, for different organs of an individual body,[12] and for different blood vessels.[13]

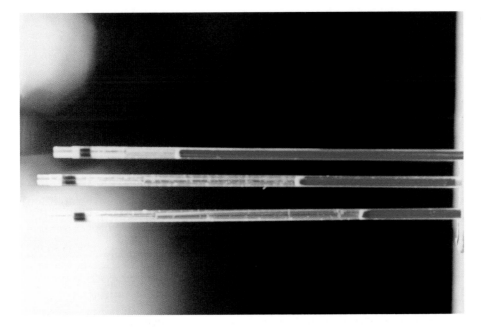

Figure 1.2

Standardized capillary tubes show variance for hematocrit of 15, 45, and 65%, bottom to top.

The relevance of hematocrit variance, in terms of an effect on viscosity, has been questioned in regard to victims of assault.[14] It should be noted that not only does considerable hematocrit variance occur for ambulatory victims, but that criminal assaults are not limited to victims who can walk. Some variations which can be found in victims of violence are shown in Table 1.1.

Red blood cells are heavier than plasma.[15] This can be seen in bodies as *lividity*, where red cells settle to the lowest extremity of a body after death. The actions of a healthy circulatory system keep red cells in motion and prevent sedimentation during life. Even blood drawn for clinical tests such as the Erythrocyte Sedimentation Rate (ESR)[16] normally shows little settling within an hour.

Table 1.1

Victims span a wide range of hematocrit ratios.

Hematocrit	Possible victims with range of hematocrit
15–29%	Chronic alcoholics and drug abusers, steroid abusers, women after traumatic child birth or illegal abortion, malnourished homeless, elderly.
30–48%	Normal range for nontraumatic venipuncture (blood drawn in a clinic or hospital) samples.
49–75%	Dehydrated individuals, people in shock, those living at high altitude, impending and active heart attack victims, newborn babies, and aborted late-term fetuses, people suffering hypothermia, and people after extreme physical exercise.

Stored blood such as out-of-date transfusion pouches, however, permit considerable settling as a response to changes in the red cells with conditions of storage. Fresh blood sedimentation may not occur before stages of coagulation and/or drying intervene to prevent it.

PROPERTIES

Blood is described as a non-Newtonian viscoelastic fluid.[17] Two components contribute to this classification: red blood cells and plasma proteins. There is a complex interaction between blood viscosity and non-Newtonian behavior, yet viscosity alone does not make a fluid non-Newtonian.[18] Glycerine is viscous but classified as Newtonian.[19] This is significant since glycerine and dye is often suggested as a safe alternative to blood for bloodstain pattern research and training. Some authors have focused on blood viscosity to understand behavior.[14] The problem with this is that blood viscosity is more complicated than non-Newtonian behavior, and an integral part of it. The two subjects can not be separated without a loss of clarity. First, blood viscosity is not constant.[20] It is dependent upon hematocrit and plasma phase viscosity, time, temperature, and shear rate.[21] Secondly, non-Newtonian fluid viscosity cannot be measured by the same methods as Newtonian fluid viscosity.[22] Technical literature reviewed expresses doubts regarding the validity of any fixed reported measurement.[23] The science which studies deformation, flow, and drop separation for such non-Newtonian materials as blood, plastics, paints, and food is rheology.[24]

Viscosity varies with time, temperature, and shear rate. Shear stress variance means blood viscosity changes depending upon what is happening to it. Thus the stress changes when one layer of a fluid flows against another surface or layer with interfacial variance. The definition has led to an assumption that shear simply concerns flow. With blood, however, characteristics of shear influences formation of all the pattern types. This will be discussed in the relevant chapters which follow. Unfortunately, no specific research has been done incorporating biorheology into Blood Dynamics. Hopefully this work will serve as an incentive for future studies.

IMPORTANCE OF NON-NEWTONIAN BEHAVIOR

Newtonian fluids include water, aqueous dyes, inks, and air while non-Newtonian fluids include egg white, mammalian blood, oils, liquid plastics, and mud.[25] Plasma and serum may be considered Newtonian[26] or non-Newtonian[27] depending in part upon behavior at the interface with air.[28] Research in blood-stain pattern analysis has focused on water drop formation reference literature.[29,30] This is understandable since a large volume of information is available relating to rain drop formation. Delay in understanding non-Newtonian behavior in general is also acknowledged by researchers in non-Newtonian fluid mechanics.[31] Newtonian behavior was defined as early as 1840 while non-Newtonian fluids were not actively studied until 1940.[32] Since Dr Paul Kirk's academic background stemmed from prior to 1939, it is reasonable to believe that he was unaware of non-Newtonian fluid behavior or that blood was classed as such.

The following list shows areas in bloodstain pattern evidence which will benefit from research in non-Newtonian fluid behavior:

- Drop separation and size determination.
- Satellite drop breakage phenomenon.
- Drop flight stability.
- Coalescence and ricochet of drops.
- *Arterial gush* pattern dynamics.
- *Blood into blood* pattern formation.
- *Physiologically altered bloodstain* appearance.
- Coagulation of blood.

Biorheology (formerly hemorheology) is the study of blood and other biological fluids as they flow within organs and vessels, natural or implanted. Rheology, however, includes the study of external *drop separation*[33] and streaming[34] of fluids comparable to blood behavior in criminal acts. Compression studies as part of non-Newtonian *shear* could be applied to blood between two surfaces, such as that between a victim and a surface being used to bludgeon them or a bullet at penetration of skin, muscle, bone, and other tissue.

Blood exhibits axial flow,[35] which is a spiral version of laminar flow and exists when different layers move at different rates. Blood drawn during medical testing involves nontraumatic venipuncture. The action of drawing blood into a syringe or vacuum test tube creates a homogeneous, evenly mixed, sample.

When blood flows normally in blood vessels, the composition is layered. Red blood cells form a spiraling core, surrounded by white blood cells, with plasma and platelets circulating around the circumference (see Figure 1.3).

Non-Newtonian flow provides stability which resists turbulence, and prevents drop separation intravascularly.[36] This means that because blood is non-Newtonian life supporting circulation in mammals is possible. Newtonian behavior would involve disrupted flow within branching blood vessels. The stability of flow influences blood behavior during violent acts. Blood requires more force to be broken into drops than Newtonian fluids. This is why blood-stain patterns can be used to reconstruct the original distributing events. Blood drops do not oscillate as do Newtonian water drops.[37] This phenomenon is due to the non-Newtonian fluid behavior of strong cohesion.

Figure 1.3

Blood shown in laminar axial flow.

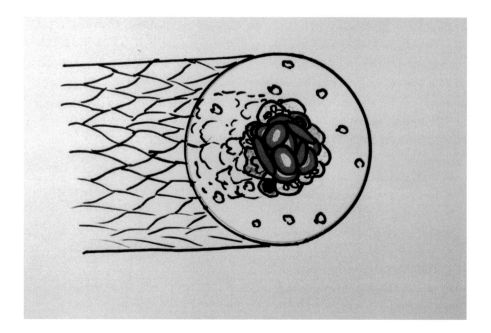

BLOOD FUNCTIONS OF INTEREST IN CRIMINAL JUSTICE

Blood has functions that provide information to many science subdivisions. From a criminal justice perspective there are four major roles:

- Oxygen transport. The brain, heart, other vital organs, and all tissue cells are supplied with oxygen by blood. Rapid blood loss causes dizziness, fainting, and death from lack of oxygen. Individuals can not function aggressively after massive blood loss even if that would be their normal disposition. Transfusion research, however, has found that giving oxygen is less efficacious than giving blood.[6]

- Fluid balance and temperature regulation. Blood loss victims must be kept warm and given replacement fluids to reduce the effects of shock.
- Transport of toxic waste products from the body. This is why color and odor suggest cause and manner of death with carbon monoxide, alcoholism, diabetic coma, and some poisoning. Blood is a primary source for drugs of abuse testing.
- Supply nourishment to body tissue. This provides information of malnutrition in alcoholics, abused children, and mistreated elderly people.

DEFINITION

With so many viewpoints regarding blood, one can find definitions ranging from the dangerously over-simplified to the hopelessly complex. Medically it is considered an organ like the brain, heart, liver, kidneys, and stomach. From the criminal justice perspective a definition of blood may be more applicable as:

> A vital, complex biological fluid, containing red blood cells, which is present in verte-brates and may be shed during accidental, intensional, and/or criminal acts.

Many other definitions may be derived for blood. The one above should serve as a suggestion for those wishing to avoid further complexity.

CLASSIFICATION OF BLOODSTAIN PATTERNS

IS IT BLOOD?

Bloodstains should always be verified with approved tests. Sampling every spot at a crime scene, however, is impractical, expensive, and unnecessary. There are also situations where crime scenes are irrevocably changed after preliminary examination. Every effort should be made to record and photograph crime scenes as early as possible. If photographs are all that remains for evaluation, an *ABC Approach to Bloodstain Verification* can improve confidence that recognized bloodstains are blood. ABC refers to:

- **A**ppearance
- **B**ehavior
- **C**ontext

APPEARANCE

Blood has distinctive color, hue, tint, and saturation. These are learned from crime scene experience and become part of an investigators' experience memory. Some approaches to color recognition are also part of forensic science.[38] The types of shine, sheen, and reflectivity for blood may be learned by those having frequent contact with the substance, either in casework, laboratories, or training workshops (see Figure 1.4).

Figure 1.4

Fresh bloodstains among drops from red colored cough suppressant liquids.

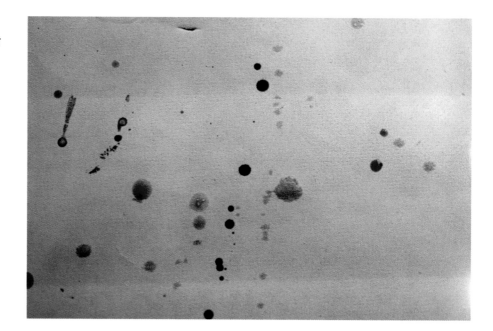

BEHAVIOR

Blood is unique and distinct from other fluids in that it can clot, separate into red cells and clear liquid, and hemolyze (to be discussed in Chapter 8). The particulate nature can be seen in a dry stain compared with clear liquid, as seen in Figure 1.5. The way it deforms when drying is also recognizable behavior (see Figure 1.6). More will be discussed about this in Chapter 8, on Physiologically Altered Blood Stains. The odor of blood results from decomposition and biochemical changes. Recognition of odors can be learned from experience.

CONTEXT

If a whole pattern containing several parts, such as impact spatters or serial transfers, is identified, all the parts of the pattern need not be separately chemically tested. A reasonable sample can be representative of the whole. What constitutes a reasonable sample should be discussed with the appropriate forensic laboratory. If a blood source is recognized by a professional such as a physician, nurse, or paramedic, flows from the same source will most likely also be blood.

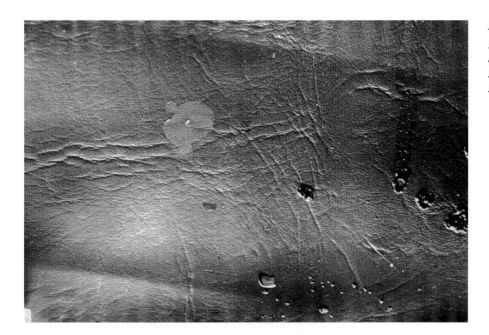

Figure 1.5

*Blood, anticoagulated,
compared with cough
syrup on a nonabsorbent
surface after 3 days.*

Figure 1.6

*Fresh blood, no anticoagu-
lant, is allowed to dry on
jeans denim fabric.*

It must be emphasized that the ABC approach will not be of use if quality color photographs and recorded observations are unavailable. Recognition of the value of bloodstain pattern evidence must apply to the crime scene as early in the investigation as possible to avoid loss of valuable physical evidence.

DEVELOPING A BLOODSTAIN PATTERN FLOW DIAGRAM

Once it is established that the substance being analyzed is blood, a division of the pattern groups is suggested on the basis of dynamics. One set of dynamics involves the distribution of drops and the other does not involve drops as a basis of pattern identification. All individual bloodstains which have resulted from blood drop distribution are called *spatter patterns*. This division will be called the *Spatter Groups*. Dr Paul Kirk recognized this division of patterns although he called spatters, spots. He labeled three dynamics which he believed could be identified from the distribution of drops during events. These are the Impact, Cast Off, and Arterial Damage categories.

A second set of dynamics can be identified where spatters, spots, are not involved in pattern identification. These include the groups of Transfers, Physiologically Altered Blood Stains (PABS), and Volume (pooled blood). Each of these groups can be differentiated into a number of specific patterns. Additionally, composites have been identified which may be applied to analysis in order to expedite interpretation. Figure 1.7 presents an outline of classifications presently identified for bloodstain patterns. All of these patterns will be discussed in the chapters which follow.

Figure 1.7

Flow diagram of blood-stain patterns.

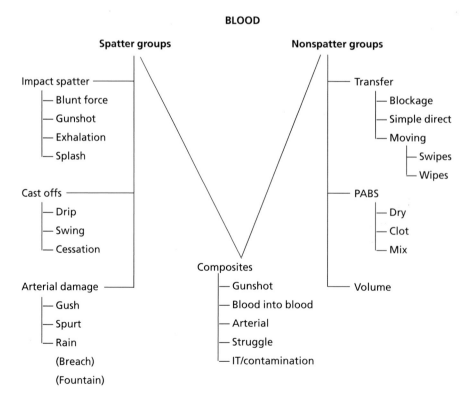

REFERENCES

1. Kirk, Paul L. (1963) *Necessary Expert Witnesses in Criminal Matters*, in Paul Kirk Papers, Bancroft Library. University of California, Berkeley, p. 153.

2. Kirk, Paul L. (1962) *The Expert Witness in Criminal Cases.* Summary of the Proceedings of the 40th Annual Conference National Legal Aid and Defender Association, San Francisco, p. 63.

3. Franklin-Barbajosa, Cassandra (May 1992) 'DNA profiling: the new science of identity'. *National Geographic* **181**(5), 112.

4. Wambaugh, Joseph (1989) *The Blooding.* William Morrow, NY, pp. 71–75.

5. Janson, H.W. (1964) *History of Art.* Prentice-Hall, New Jersey, and Harry N. Abrams, New York, p. 18.

6. Allen, Robert W., Kahn, Richard A. and Baldassare, Joseph J. (1986) 'Advances in the production of blood cell substitutes with alternative technologies', in *New Frontiers in Blood Banking* (eds C.H. Wallas and L.J. McCarthy). American Association of Blood Banks, Washington, DC, p. 22.

7. Whitmore, R.L. (1968) *Rheology of the Circulation.* Pergamon Press, Oxford, p. 61.

8. Hein, Morris, Best, Leo R., Pattison, Scott and Arena, Susan (1993) *College Chemistry an Introduction to General, Organic, and Biochemistry* (5th edn). Brooks/Cole, Pacific Grove, CA, pp. 387–391.

9. Dailey, John F. (1998) *Blood.* Medical Consulting Group. Arlington, Massachusetts.

10. Nelson, Douglas A. and Rodak, Bernadette F. (1983) 'Hematology', in *Clinical Guide to Laboratory Tests* (Ed. Norbert W. Tietz). WB Saunders. Philadelphia, pp. 258–259.

11. Nelson, Douglas A. and Morris, Michael W. (1991) 'Basic examination of blood', in *Clinical Diagnosis and Management by Laboratory Methods* (18th edn) (Ed. John Bernard Henry). WB Saunders. Philadelphia, p. 598.

12. Albert, Solomon N. (1971) *Blood Volume and Extracellular Fluid Volume* (2nd edn). Charles C. Thomas, Springfield, IL, p. 50.

13. *Ibid*, p. 49.

14. Bevel, Tom and Gardner, Ross M. (1997) *Bloodstain Pattern Analysis with an Introduction to Crime Scene Reconstruction.* CRC, Boca Raton, FL, p. 77.

15. Chmiel, Horst and Walitza, Eckehard (1980) *On the Rheology of Blood and Synovial Fluids.* John Wiley and Sons, London, p. 6.

16. Tietz, Norbert W. (Ed.) (1983) *Clinical Guide to Laboratory Tests.* WB Saunders, Philadelphia, p. 176.

17. Lowe, Gordon D.O. (1988) *Clinical Blood Rheology Vol. I* (Ed Gordon D.O. Lowe). CRC, Boca Raton, FL, p. 5.

18. *Ibid*, p. 4.

19. Boger, D.V. and Walters, K. (1993) *Rheological Series 4, Rheological Phenomena in Focus.* Elsevier, Amsterdam, p. 130.

20. Lowe, Gordon D.O. (1988) *op. cit.*, p. 5.

21. *Ibid,* p. 26.

22. Walters, Kenneth (1975) *Rheometry.* Chapman and Hall. London, p. 2.

23. Whorlow, R.W. (1992) *Rheological Techniques* (2nd edn). Ellis Horwood, New York, p. 11.

24. Vennard, John K. and Street, Robert L. (1982) *Elementary Fluid Mechanics* (6th edn). John Wiley and Sons. New York, p. 16.

25. Selby, M.J. (1985) *The Earth's Changing Surface, an Introduction to Geomorphology.* Clarendon Press. Oxford, p. 175.

26. Lowe, Gordon D.O. (1988) *op. cit.*, p. 280.

27. Hyman, W.A. and Skalak, R. (1970) *Viscous Flow of a Suspension of Deformable Liquid Drops in a Cylindrical Tube.* Columbia University, New York, p. 1.

28. Lowe, Gordon D.O. (1988) *op. cit.*, p. 18.

29. Raymond, Anthony, Smith, E.R. and Liesegang, J. (1996) 'Oscillating blood droplets – implications for crime scene reconstruction'. *Science and Justice* **36**(3), 161–171.

30. Pizzola, P.A., Roth, Steven and DeForest, Peter (1986) 'Blood droplet dynamics – I and II'. *Journal of Forensic Sciences* **31**(1), 36–64.

31. Tanner, R.I. and Walters, Kenneth (1998) *Rheology: An Historical Perspective.* Elsevier, Amsterdam, p. vii.

32. Nubar, Yves (1966) *The Laminar Flow of a Composite Fluid: an Approach to the Rheology of Blood.* New York Academy of Sciences, NY, p. 35.

33. Bürkholz, Armin (1989) *Droplet Separation.* Verlagsgesellschaft, Republic of Germany.

34.   Boger, David V. and Walters, Kenneth (1993) *Rheological Series 4: Rheological Phenomena in Focus.* Elsevier, London, p. 138.

35.   Tullis, James L. (1976) *Clot.* Charles C. Thomas. Springfield, IL, pp. 66–67.

36.   Bockchoon, Pak, Young, I. Cho and Choi, Steven U.S. (1990) 'Separation and reattachment of non-Newtonian fluid flows in sudden expansion pipe'. *Journal of Non-Newtonian Fluid Mechanics* **37**(5), 175–199.

37.   Bevel, Tom and Gardner, Ross M. (1997) *op. cit.*, p. 82.

38.   Houck, Max M. (2000) 'What is color? How is it perceived?', in *Color Analysis in Forensic Science Workshop.* AAFS 52nd Annual Meeting. Reno, Nevada.

All of the major spatter groups are represented, yet this scene was labeled simply
'Medium Velocity Impact Spatter'

CHAPTER 2

INTRODUCTION TO THE SPATTER GROUPS

DEVELOPING TERMINOLOGY

In 1963, Dr Paul Kirk compiled a paper entitled 'Blood Spot Analysis for the California Trial Lawyers Association'. In it he discussed the use of 'blood spots' in criminal investigations.[1,2] He described two characteristics of bloodstains which he considered essential to interpretation:

- The size of the individual spots.
- Speed (velocity) of drops at impact with a recording surface.

A phrase used by Dr Kirk in his testimonies and research to describe the 'spots' was *velocity impact spatter*. He equated relative blood drop speed to recorded spot, *spatter*, appearance. This was consistent with earlier studies in France by Balthazard *et al.*,[3] and earlier still in Poland by Piotrowski.[4] During Kirk's tenure, 1939–1970, measuring actual velocities for individual blood drops was infeasible. The phrase, therefore, was applied as general comparative terms rather than precise numerical values. Drops free falling by gravity alone were considered *low velocity*. They would contact a surface (now called a *target*) with a *low velocity impact* leaving stains which were labeled *low velocity impact spatter*. Drops contacting a target at *medium velocity* left *medium velocity impact spatter*, and drops distributed at *high velocities* left *high velocity impact spatter*. *Impact* only referred to a blood drop hitting a target surface.

As a measure of the relative velocity for a blood drop, calculations were later suggested based on *terminal velocity*.[5] An object in free fall will accelerate due to the forces of gravity while pushing against air resistance until an equilibrium is reached. After that point free fall will be at constant velocity.[6] This information was given for blood drops of unknown hematocrit as 25.1 feet per second with a degree of error of ±0.5 feet per second;[7] It was also accepted that drops of different size would have different terminal velocities. Terminal velocity is a factor in the spread of drops recorded after free fall.[8] This results in spatter size variance as seen in Figure 2.1.

Since hematocrits affect the mass of blood drops, and mass influences

Figure 2.1

Three drops each of 10 microliters (left) and 50 microliters (right) fell 8 feet on to metal.

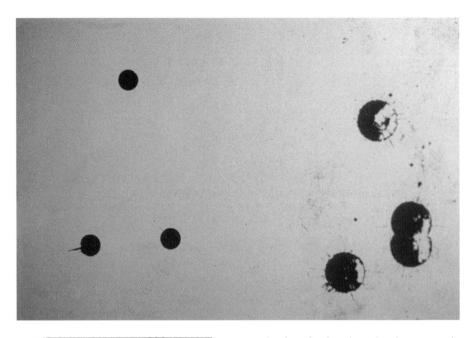

Figure 2.2

Drops of 15, 45, and 65% (top to bottom) hematocrit fell 6, 12, and 24 inches on to fine grain sandpaper. Edge characteristics demonstrate red blood cell cohesion.

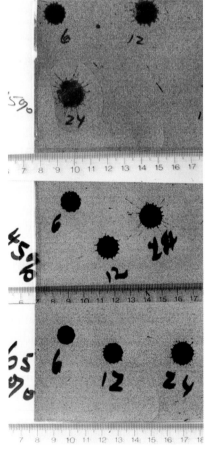

terminal velocity in air, hematocrit variance will influence terminal velocities. No data has previously been formally presented regarding this relationship. Figure 2.2 provides an indication of the types of differences red cell concentration will have on bloodstain appearance after free fall.

Dr Kirk identified individual stain characteristics which he associated with relative drop velocities. *Low velocity impact spatters* were large, round or slightly oval, with smooth or nearly smooth circumferences. This was later modified to include surface textures of the target.[9,10] Rough surfaces resulted in spiked circumferences while smooth hard targets recorded smooth edges. *Medium velocity impact spatters* were medium sized, although no exact size was listed, shaped like bowling pins with their smallest end located in the *Direction of Travel* of the blood drop at impact with the target. *High velocity*

Impact Spatters included drops that resembled exclamation marks and ellipses with *satellite (secondary) spatter* fanning out from the *parent drop* like a fish tail.

Sometime after 1970, the meaning of velocity impact spatter (VIS) was shifted to define velocity of an object 'impacting' a blood source[11] which then distributes drops. A medium velocity impact (MVI) was one which received a force of 25 feet per second, associated with bludgeoning,[12] while a high velocity impact (HVI) was defined as 100 feet per sec,[13] associated with a gunshot. This shift in meaning has created confusion and controversy, especially since impact could now refer to either the victim (blood source) or the target. In the case of Low Velocity Impact Spatter (LVIS) from drops which fell by the force of gravity alone, distribution does not result from an impact, so the LVIS term became a misnomer. Medium and High Velocity Impacts occur, but the velocity is not measured at the spatter position (on the target), making MVI spatter and HVI spatter ambiguous terms. This terminology has been questioned and debated internationally for many years.[14] Since bloodstain pattern evidence began with infrequent use, this was not a problem. Unfortunately, expanding applications, training, research, science principles, and standardized terms for court makes ambiguous terminology less acceptable.

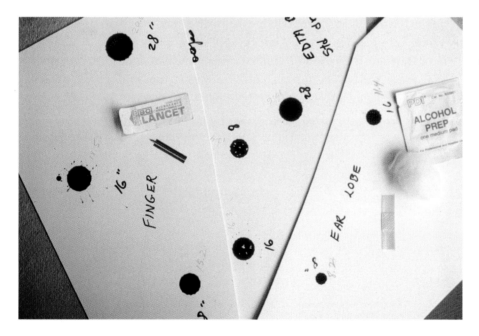

Figure 2.3

Drops were allowed to free fall from long point lancet cuts to a finger (left) and an ear lobe (right). These are compared with a theoretical standard sized drop of 50 microliters (center).

A standard drop size was defined as 0.05 cm^3 with 95% confidence limits.[15] For the purposes of a study a single drop can be suggested within the limits of experimentation, but validity in a crime context does not necessarily follow. Figure 2.3 shows blood drops from standardized cuts to the finger and ear lobe compared with a 0.05 cm³ (50 microliter) drop. If standardized injuries do not relate to the same size drop, given all the variations in hematocrit possible, a standard size drop cannot be estimated for a crime scene.

Further development of the concept equated dynamic acts with theoretical break up of the standard sized drop. Dripping blood would be 'full sized drops', beating blows would break up drops into medium size droplets, and gunshot might break up a drop into mist. The primary problem here is that there is no such thing as a standard sized drop. The size of blood drops at crime scenes will depend on the blood source, blood composition, type and degree of force, and dynamics of drop separation. These cannot be standardized for crimes and/or crime scenes. Therefore, if there is no such thing as a standard size drop, no classification scheme based upon the break up of that drop is valid.

Different dynamic acts also distribute drops of different sizes with considerable size range overlap.[16] No single spatter size is exclusive to the designated 'velocity' of an impact. Spatters labeled medium and high velocity impact spatter may occur from actions other than impacts such as those thrown off rapidly moving objects (Cast Offs) and sprayed from high pressured blood vessels (Arterial Damage patterns). Further, the concept of terminal velocity has been retained with the implication that this applies to *spatters*. Terminal velocity relates to a blood drop in free fall due to gravity alone, not to drops distributed by force. Terminal velocity can not be applied to Impact, Swing Cast Off, or Arterial Damage. It can only be applied to dripping blood, i.e. drip cast offs.

The numerical values for velocities, individual stain sizes and distances traveled for velocity impact spatters, have been demonstrated by a centripetal

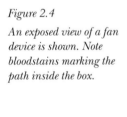

Figure 2.4

An exposed view of a fan device is shown. Note bloodstains marking the path inside the box.

(cast off), not an impact, principle. A device, similar to the one shown in Figure 2.4, is constructed with rubber blades attached to the drive shaft of a motor, encased in a box with two holes, top and side, set to spin at a measurable rate, (RPM). A quantity of blood, usually 2 to 5 cm^3, is dropped into the top hole, with drops projected out the side toward a strip of butcher paper or arrangement of cardboard sheets. The principle is flawed in a number of ways. The velocity of the blades is not set at the threshold of adhesion between blood and blade surface. The threshold would determine when drop separation could occur under the conditions of the experiment. The common device uses a single speed motor where rotation is at some velocity higher than a drop separation threshold. The size and distance traveled by specific blood spatters cannot be equated to the single measured rotational speed in this situation. The conclusion from the fan device exercise can only state that spatters of the size and distance traveled resulted from a velocity equal to or less than the measured speed of the fan blades. The device does show linear distribution of drop sizes for a specific composition of blood.

Limitations of the fan design also involve the nature of blood used, as well as that of the blades themselves. Since the threshold depends on breaking the adhesion of the blood coating the blades, the strength of adhesion must be considered. Nonwettable surfaces, such as teflon and plexiglas, permit drop separation more readily than wood, rubber, or paper. The amount and composition of blood must be considered. Red cells provide additional mass as well as cohesion which means the depth of a coating layer affects the threshold at which blood drops will separate. On the basis of this, information gleaned thus far from fan devices is irrelevant with regard to crime scene evidence. Case reports, however, are encountered where gunshot distributed spatter is identified because of size and distance traveled assumed from data collected from fan device experimentation. One cannot use a cast off method to identify impact dynamics.

Some investigators have attempted to resolve the ambiguity of VIS terms by claiming that spatters only result from impact. Other dynamics such as Cast Off and Arterial Damage distribute drops which are not called spatters.[17] This would be acceptable if spots from Impact could be immediately differentiated from spots distributed by other dynamics. Unfortunately, neither size nor shape can be applied as exclusive to Impact, and the products of other dynamics frequently overlap Impact patterns. Limiting the term spatter to Impact dynamics leads investigators to classify all spots as resulting from Impact. In the Frontispiece all of the main spatter groups are illustrated yet some investigators classified them all as Medium Velocity Impact Spatters. Differentiation into different pattern types was not recorded. It is expedient to call all spots spatters, then apply objective criteria to differentiate them into Impact, Cast Off, or Arterial Damage. This format is also consistent with the approach suggested by Paul Kirk.

Too often spatters are labeled on the basis of crime events rather than blood-stain characteristics. For example, a student viewed an *arterial spurt* pattern in an examination. The question asked: 'What would you call this pattern found at the scene of death by handgun?' The student circled, 'High Velocity Impact Spatter'. When asked why that answer was chosen, he responded with, 'You said it was a handgun'. This type of subjective application is common with velocity impact spatter terminology.

Although the velocity impact spatter terms as originally described by Dr Kirk have application in the examination of bloodstain pattern evidence, the controversies which currently exist suggest a need for more specific and concise terminology with regard to general spatter descriptions. This can be accomplished within existing semantics. In fact in a presentation from 1968, Dr Kirk outlined the direction research should take in this discipline:

> One other type of information that is most helpful and greatly neglected is the analysis of blood distribution at the scene of a violent crime. The hydrodynamics of flying blood drops has received very little attention, although *numerous discussions of angle and velocity of single drops are available.* The general pattern is actually far more informative and, in favorable cases, is by far the most significant evidence available for the detailed reconstruction of the activities of both the assailant and the victim during the critical moments of the commission of the crime.
>
> Blood which is thrown during the crime shows definite regularities as to size and velocity of the drops, which will differ depending on whether the drops receive their velocity from *impact, from being thrown [cast off] from a bloody weapon as it swings, or from spurting of a severed artery.* These *patterns* are not only different, but show characteristic patterns that can often be recognized. Disregard of this rather obvious source of information has lessened the total information obtained by investigators of many serious crimes and is well worthy of more study and of greatly increased utilization as an investigative function.[18] [emphasis added]

It is possible to follow Dr Kirk's recommendation by first grouping spatter patterns according to primary dynamics of Impact, Cast Off, or Arterial Damage. These terms are currently used and need not cause controversy. Once the major group is recognized, further classification can be described in terms of size and characteristics such as comparing medium velocity Impact versus medium velocity Cast Off, or medium velocity versus high velocity Arterial Spurt. To avoid the original confusion of where the velocity is measured relative to spatter record, it is strongly recommended that Velocity Impact *Spatter* terms be avoided.

CLASS CHARACTERISTICS

Although spatter patterns are often emphasized over other bloodstains, they essentially involve *class characteristics*. Details from physical evidence examination can be lumped into two broad categories, *class characteristics* and *individualizing features*.[19] Class characteristics are those features which separate a class or group of like items from other classes or groups. For example a 'motor vehicle' is seen striking a pedestrian. Without a description, the individual vehicle cannot be identified. Supplying make, model, and color puts the vehicle in a class of many but excludes other makes, models, and colors. Individualizing characteristics such as the license number and/or description of dents, paint patches, and material from the victim help locate the exact vehicle involved. Bloodspatter patterns are class characteristics which can be grouped as separate acts, but each can result from many different events, not all of which are criminal.

Bloodspatters serve as a record that blood drops intercepted a recording surface, referred to as a *target*. A single spatter does not tell us where it came from, nor how it came to be distributed. It cannot be differentiated on the basis of size and shape alone from spatters resulting from different dynamics (see Figure 2.5). All spatters have common class characteristics of:

- Some kind of force was applied to a blood source.
- A blood source was separated into drops.
- Separated drops were distributed over flight paths.

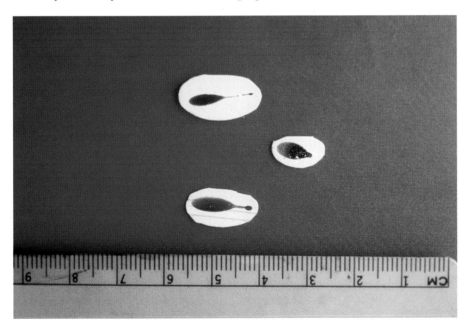

Figure 2.5

The three blood stains shown resulted from different dynamic acts: impact, cast off, and arterial spurt. See the end of Chapter 5 for answers to which group each belongs.

DROP SEPARATION

BLOOD SOURCE

Whole bloodspatter patterns are composed of groups of spatters. A single blood drop is a basic component for the formation of a spatter pattern. The first requirement is a blood source. Three categories of blood source exists:

- Injuries.
- Wet bloodstains.
- Volume accumulation.

An example of drop separation is that from wound seepage. Blood is pushed along venous blood vessels by volume behind and removal ahead of the flow. When a cut occurs, blood oozes out at a rate dependent on the volume, flow, and nature of the injured vessel. The nature of injuries and details of bleeding are the expertise of medical doctors, yet understanding bloodstain patterns requires some attention to the blood source. Investigators must interact with physicians in order to fully understand both blood sources and bloodstain patterns.

SURFACE TENSION VERSUS COHESION

Traditionally drop formation is defined in terms of *surface tension*,[20] the membrane-like invisible force that holds a drop in a rounded shape on a surface or in flight. Newtonian fluids, such as water, form drops depending upon the strength of the surface tension and weight of the drop formed. Non-Newtonian fluids such as blood are more affected by viscosity and internal cohesion than by surface tension. Viscosity of blood determines a dynamic (sometimes referred to as the apparent) surface tension. In textbooks on non-Newtonian fluid mechanics surface tension is seldom, if ever, mentioned.[21] Blood holds a rounded shape because of the strong internal *cohesion* created by red blood cells. Figure 2.6 shows a blood drop holding shape and contact with the blood source against gravitational pull. Cohesion is influenced by the red cell ratio, hematocrit. Surface tension acts only on the surface, while cohesion acts throughout the fluid.[22] Even a fluid with a stronger surface tension such as water is considerably weaker than blood's cohesion. See Figure 2.7 for a pictorial representation of the two forces.

Figure 2.6
Internal cohesion of blood is strong enough to hold the developing drop to the blood source, injury to the finger.

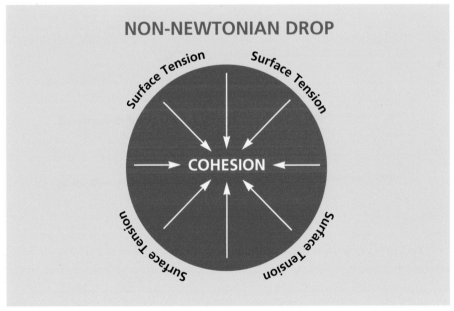

Figure 2.7
Surface tension only acts on the surface of a drop. Cohesion acts throughout and in the case of blood creates a much stronger bond.

NON-NEWTONIAN BEHAVIOR

The fact that blood is non-Newtonian provides advantages and disadvantages for pattern formation. An advantage is that non-Newtonian behavior imparts a greater stability to fluid flows and drops. The wobble seen with Newtonian drops does not occur to the same degree with non-Newtonian drops.[23] Figure 2.8 illustrates comparisons between Newtonian and various types of non-

Newtonian fluid drops separating from streams.[24] Notice the flattening and apparent increase in diameter of Newtonian drops subjected to air resistance. Non-Newtonian fluid drops may demonstrate a short span of equilibrium adjustment when a drop breaks free, but motion is predominantly confined to one plane, up and down.[25]

Figure 2.8

Examples of flow characteristics for Newtonian (a, b), non-Newtonian inelastic (c), and non-Newtonian viscoelastic (d–g) fluids. Blood behaves as a viscoelastic non-Newtonian fluid.[a] Reprinted by permission of Elsevier publishers.

[a]Chemical compositions of fluids shown are: A) 75% aqueous glycerine, B) ethylene glycol, C) 0.1% Carbopol, D) 0.05% Separan, E) 0.25% Separan, F) 0.25% Polyox, and G) 25% carboxymethyl cellulose.

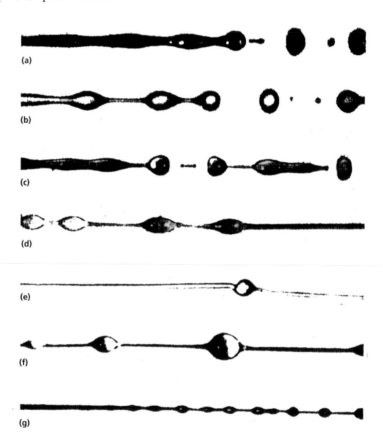

(a)

(b)

(c)

(d)

(e)

(f)

(g)

A disadvantage with non-Newtonian behavior is that describing drop separation is much more technical than traditional surface tension models (see references listed for applicable physics and mathematics formulae). When force overcomes the viscosity and internal cohesion of the non-Newtonian fluid, drops will separate. Viscosity and internal cohesion, which are influenced and increased by higher hematocrits, attempt to keep a blood source together. More force is necessary for blood drops to separate than to form drops from Newtonian fluid, such as water (Figures 2.9 and 2.10).

The uniqueness of non-Newtonian blood in pattern analysis is useful. Bloodstain patterns result according to science principles beyond simple physics. What happens in an area of space will be recorded on surfaces in predictable

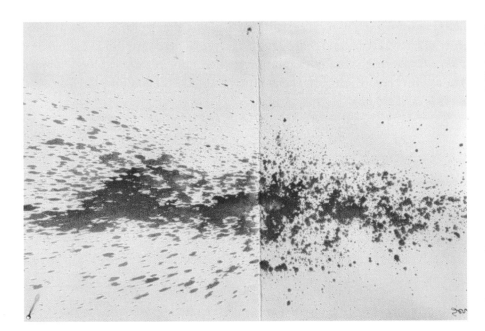

Figure 2.9

One cubic centimeter of sea water with dye, specific gravity of 1.030, subjected to spring trap impact.

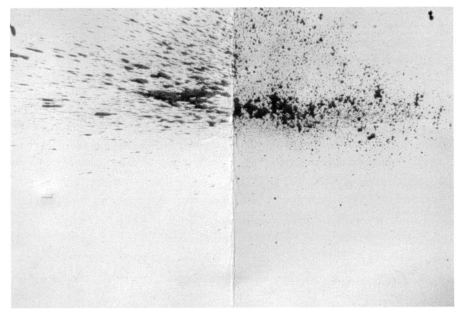

Figure 2.10

Two cubic centimeters of 55% hematocrit blood, subjected to the same conditions of impact.

and reproducible patterns. Water and other Newtonian fluids do not leave records of dynamic events in the same manner as blood.

In the 1980s researchers discovered that blood does not flow homogeneously (evenly) mixed within blood vessels.[26] Instead they found that flow is laminar. When injury occurs, two events follow: the injured blood vessels constrict[27] and flow is disrupted. A schematic representation is shown in Figure 2.11. Although it has not been published, observations were made by some physicians that

[b]Discussion with medical residents at Sacramento Medical Foundation Blood Bank.

blood alcohol levels in trauma victims may not be affected by multiple transfusions of packed red blood cells.[b] This suggests that in some traumatic situations red cells may be lost out of proportion to their ratio in a whole blood sample. These observations are consistent with vessel constriction and laminar flow models of blood loss.

Figure 2.11

When injury occurs to a blood vessel, constriction follows. Observations suggest red cells are then lost out of proportion to their hematocrit in the blood vessel.

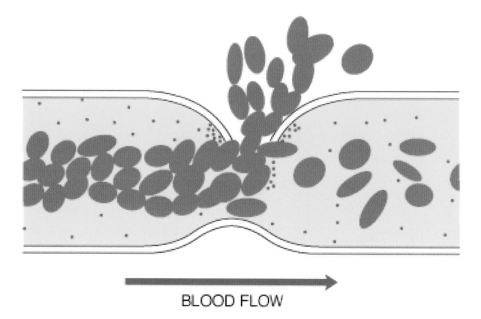

BLOOD FLOW

The effect of increased red cells is that smaller drops will have greater mass but also greater cohesion. Smaller drops will separate but require more force to do so. Two crime scene observations indicate that drops from criminal violence are concentrated in red cells: bloodstains at crime scenes are often very dark in color, and workshop experiments are closer to actual casework when packed cell transfusion units are used. The darker color indicates a greater density of red cells than present in whole blood samples.

BLOOD SPATTER SIZES

A range of blood spatter sizes will be encountered during crime scene investigation. Since the pattern group may not be immediately identified, spatter sizes should be noted and recorded. Size ranges have been suggested by investigators experienced in both crime scenes and training programs:[28]

- *Mist:* spatters which are less than 0.1 mm in diameter.
- *Fine:* spatters which are greater than 0.1 but less than 1 mm in diameter.
- *Small:* spatters which are greater than 1 but less than 3 mm in diameter.

- *Medium:* spatters which are greater than 3 but less than 6 mm in diameter.
- *Large:* spatters which are greater than 6 mm in diameter.[c]

An undifferentiated pattern consisting of a predominance of any one sized spatter can be referred to as that *size spatter pattern*, i.e. a pattern of predominant stains less than 0.1 mm in diameter can be referred to as a mist spatter pattern. Fine and mist are often confused. A guideline is that individual fine spatters may be visible with the unaided eye, while individual mist spatters are not. A mist pattern usually appears spray painted, and thus becomes visible from the density, number, of spatters present.

[c]These terms are recommended at present, but future evaluation may modify or alter them.

DIRECTION OF TRAVEL

After the blood drop separates it forms a sphere which is distributed over some kind of flight path. When it encounters a target it will leave a record in the form of a bloodspatter (or spatter). Although we may not immediately know what dynamic act distributed the blood drop, we can usually determine in which direction a drop was traveling prior to target contact.

A drop of blood falling or projected directly down will contact the target at right angles and leave a stain that is a cross section of a sphere. Dissipation of momentum from fall will be equal around the stain. Depending on the drop size and surface texture of the target, protuberances and spines may be recorded around the circumference. If direction of travel was perpendicular to the target, the spines should be of equal size and distribution. If the drop met the target at an angle with direction of travel other than 90°, the spines will be longer or more distinctive in that direction. In theory, drops meeting the target at right angles will be completely round, while drops meeting at angles will be ellipses with the longer measurement along the line of travel.

If drops behaved strictly according to the theoretical model, spatters would show only the line of travel, not from/to directionality. What actually occurs with a blood drop meeting a target at an angle other than 90° is that forward momentum is not all dissipated at contact. A portion of the drop, which meets the target first, stops movement and stains the surface. Fluid not in contact with the target continues travel, but there is less substance since some is left as stain. This results in a narrowing of the spatter in the direction of travel. Target surface effects will cause variations, especially in the leading edge of the spatter.

It is unwise to base direction of travel on measurements alone. Uneven absorbent material will shorten or elongate spatters based more on the target characteristics than the direction of travel. The guideline for determining direction of travel is to regard travel as in *the direction of the greatest edge distortion*. See Figure 2.12 for examples.

Figure 2.12

Various examples of leading edge characteristics are shown.

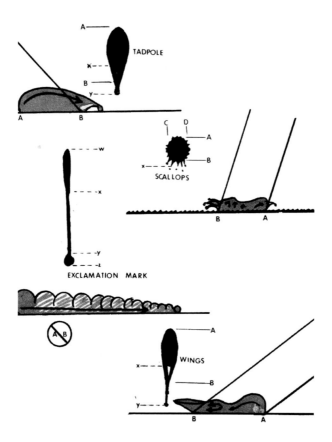

Because drops do not make contact with the target in the same manner as a theoretical model, the cross section of the blood drop does not leave a perfect oval shape. This permits us to determine the direction of travel, but it presents a problem with measurements. The steeper, narrower, the angle the drop hits the target, the greater the problem with measurements. The faster the drop is traveling, using Dr Kirk's approach to spatters, the less cross sectional contact it makes when it touches the target. This means that making the stain into a perfect oval to determine the length will cut the stain too short, and make the angle more open than indicated by the actual drop contact with the surface. Although filling out an oval seems logical with angles near 90°, at narrower angles the problems become clear. See Figure 2.13 for an example of drop over flow at contact with a target.

Fortunately this is unimportant in processing impact spatters at crime scenes. Drip cast off spatters are affected by falling on a slant because of the amount of blood in the drop. When contact is made and travel continues, there is excess blood to deposit. Drops separated from the blood source by force are broken up. The smaller drops have less blood, thus are more likely to make a complete

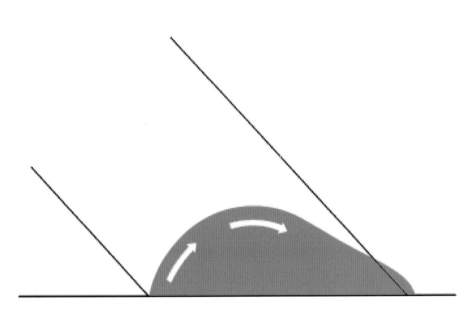

Figure 2.13
A drop hitting a target at
an angle does not make
complete cross-section
contact.

contact when hitting a target. Complete contact means all or most of the drop is deposited at once. Measuring the stains is much easier and the calculated angles are more reliable.

Although direction of travel is often applied to individual drop distribution, there are actually three ways to apply the information:

- Direction a drop traveled at impact.
- Direction an action traveled which distributed drops.
- Direction a victim traveled while an artery projected drops.

The second and third will be discussed in the relevant chapters to follow.

OBJECTIVE CRITERIA APPROACH TO SPATTER IDENTIFICATION

A compilation of factors from thousands of observations during research, workshop, and casework situations has shown that some features can be defined and applied to understand and predict the flight paths involved with drop arrays. These are presented as an objective approach to differentiating blood-spatter patterns:

Shapes of the whole pattern
Alignment of spatters with regard to whole pattern
Alignment of spatters with regard to other spatters
Distribution of sizes
Distribution of numbers of spatters

These can be abbreviated **SAADD** for a memory key. Each will be described in turn in the specific group chapters which follow.

REFERENCES

1.   Kirk, Paul Leland (1968) *Blood Spot Analysis.* Presentation Notes for Lecture at 4th Annual Criminal Law Seminar, San Francisco. Paul Kirk Papers, UC Bancroft Library, Berkeley.

2.   Kirk, Paul Leland (1967) *Blood – a Neglected Criminalistics Research Area, Law Enforcement. Science and Technology* (Ed. S.A.Yefsky). Academic Press, London, p. 271.

3.   Balthazard, V., Piedelievre, R., Desoille, H. and DeRobert, L. (1939) Etude des gouttes de sang projecte. Presented at the 22nd Congress of Forensic Medicine, Paris, France.

4.   Piotrowski, Eduard (1992) *Ueber Entstehung, Form, Richtung u. Ausbreitung der Blutduren nach Hiebwunden des Kopfes.* Golos Printing, Elmira, NY.

5.   MacDonell, Herbert Leon and Bialousz, Lorraine Fiske (1971) *Flight Characteristic and Stain Patterns of Human Blood.* US Department of Justice, Washington DC, p. 4.

6.   Sears, Francis Weston and Zemansky, Mark W. (1961) *University Physics.* Complete Edition. Addison-Wesley Publishing, Reading, Massachusetts, p. 251.

7.   MacDonell, Herbert Leon (1983) *Bloodstain Pattern Interpretation.* Laboratory of Forensic Science, Corning, NY, p. 3.

8.   Bevel, Tom and Gardner, Ross M. (1997) *Bloodstain Pattern Analysis with an Introduction to Crime Scene Reconstruction.* CRC, Boca Raton, FL, p. 94.

9.   MacDonell, Herbert L. and Bialouz, Lorraine Fiske (1971) *Op. cit.*, p. 5.

10. Kirk, Paul L. (1974) 'Blood: physical investigation', in *Crime Investigation* (2nd edn) (Ed. John I. Thornton). John Wiley and Sons, Philadelphia, p. 172.

11. MacDonell, Herbert Leon.(1991) Inquiry held under section 475 of the Crimes Act 1900 into the conviction of Alexander Lindsay (formerly Alexander McLeod-Lindsay), 28 May. Australia Federal Court, Sydney, Australia. Decided July 1991, p. 941.

12. James, Stuart H. and Eckert, William (1989) *Interpretation of Bloodstain Evidence at Crime Scenes.* Elsevier, Amsterdam, p. 52.

13. *Ibid*, p. 59.

14. *Ibid*, p. 331.

15. MacDonell, Herbert L. and Bialouz, Lorraine Fisk (1971) *Op. cit.*, p. 3.

16. Laber, Terry (1986) 'Diameter of a bloodstain as a function of origin, distance fallen, and volume of drop'. *IABPA News* **12**(1), 12–16.

17. Bevel, Tom and Gardner, Ross M. (1997) *Op. cit.*, p. 55.

18. Kirk, Paul Leland (1968) *Blood Spot Analysis.* Presentation Notes for Lecture at 4th Annual Criminal Law Seminar, San Francisco. Paul Kirk Papers, UC Bancroft Library, Berkeley, pp. 12–13.

19. Saferstein, Richard (1990) *Criminalistics: An Introduction to Forensic Science* (4th edn). Prentice Hall, Englewood Cliffs, New Jersey, p. 50.

20. Bevel, Tom and Gardner, Ross M. (1997) *Op. cit.*, p. 82.

21. Sadhal, S.S., Ayyaswamy, P. S. and Chung, J. N. (1997) *Transport Phenomena with Drops and Bubbles.* Springer. New York, p. 43.

22. White, Harvey E. (1962) *Modern College Physics* (4th edn). D. Van Nostrand, Princeton, NJ, p. 187.

23. Bevel, Tom and Gardner, Ross M. (1997) *Op. cit.*, p. 85.

24. Boger, David V. and Walters, Kenneth (1993) *Rheological Phenomenon in Focus.* Elsevier, London, p. 130.

25. *Blood in Slow Motion* (1993) Video from High Speed Movie Film. Home Office Main Laboratory, London.

26. Tullis, James L. (1976) *Clot.* Charles C. Thomas. Springfield, IL, pp. 66–67.

27. Sohmer, Paul R. (1979) 'The pathophysiology of hemorrhagic shock', in *Hemotherapy in Trauma and Surgery.* AABB, Washington, DC, p. 2.

28. Laber, Terry L. and Epstein, Barton P. (1983) *Experiments and Practical Exercises in Bloodstain Pattern Analysis.* Callan Publishing, Minneapolis, Minnesota, p. 105.

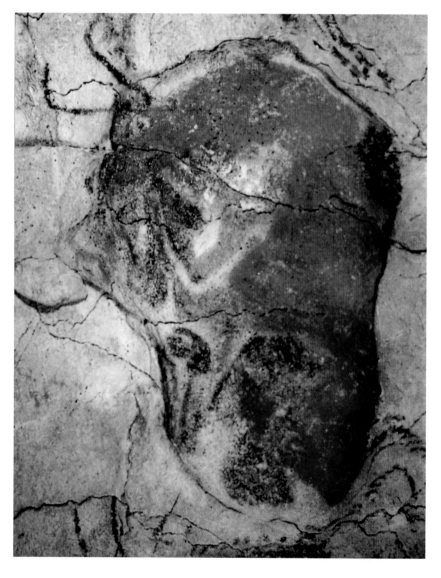

Wounded bison (13,000–15,000 B.C.), cave painting at Alta Mira, Spain.

CHAPTER 3

IMPACT SPATTER PATTERNS

The frontispiece (opposite) shows a painting on the ceiling of a Paleolithic cave. The artist applied many small spots around the head and front part of the figure. This suggests a form of Impact Spatter projected by explosive exhalation. It is possible that prehistoric man recognized the mortality of wounded animals associated with blood spatters.

DESCRIPTION OF DYNAMICS

Whether it is called energy,[1] force,[2] impulse,[3] or inertia[4] matters a great deal in terms of physics formula derivations, yet means little to applications in the field. In the case of an impact spatter pattern something caused blood drops to separate from a blood source and be distributed over an array of flight paths to leave characteristic bloodstains, called spatters. The term impact spatters is applied to those spatters which have resulted from an impact to a blood source. Arguments have been presented for the use of all four terms:

Energy   Those applying simple physics to describe events which disperse blood drops often use the kinetic energy equation,[5] $KE = \frac{1}{2} mv^2$, where m is the mass of an object striking a blood source and v is the velocity it is traveling *at* impact.[6] The rationale is that what causes blood drop distribution is equated with *work*, or the capacity to do work as in the *capacity to cause tissue damage*. As with all science equations, some assumptions are made in justifying the formula application. The source of the impact with the blood source at constant velocity is accompanied by an equal and opposite reaction in the tissue injured (Newton's Third Law of Motion). The common act of beating, however, rarely involves a weapon moving at constant velocity. Another assumption is that velocity is the primary factor in damage, thus is squared in the energy formula. Practical experience has shown this to be less applicable than other parameters.

Force   Other investigators have described acts during violent crimes in terms of Newton's Second Law of Motion, which states: *the rate of change of linear momentum is proportional to the force applied, and takes place in the straight line in* *which that force acts.*[7] In other words, the force applied will transfer effects in terms of damage. The formula used is F = ma, where m is again the mass of an object causing an impact and a is the acceleration (or deceleration) at and following impact. This deals with the two assumptions necessary with the energy formula. We are no longer concerned with constant motion and we can consider what happens immediately after impact. This formula seems to fit some impact dynamics better than the energy equation.

An example is found in gunshot Impact Spatter patterns. Different shaped ammunition can be found which carry the same mass and be projected out of a handgun at the same initial muzzle velocity. The shape of the missiles may vary from pointed, rounded, flat (dumdum), and hollow point. The resultant blood-spatter patterns following a bullet transverse of a blood source relate to the bullet differences. The more the bullet stops, the more force is transferred to tissue.[1] Pointed missiles may not slow, and thus distribute few blood drops. Rounded bullets slow somewhat and distribute more blood than pointed ones. Hollow points stop in the victim and produce considerable bloodspatters.

If this were all that we needed to consider it would solve our problem with defining impacts. Used here, impact refers to the meeting between a force and a blood source. Unfortunately science principles from one field do not always apply directly to a different field. Our biggest concern is that the change in velocity which is the acceleration/deceleration of our equation cannot be easily measured. If a factor in the equation cannot be measured, it cannot be used in an applicable science definition. Fortunately there are ways around this.

Impulse   Following Newton's Second Law of Motion which states: *the rate at which the momentum of a body changes is proportional to the impressed force and takes place in the direction of the straight line in which the force acts,*[8] the impulse equation becomes $Ft = mv - mv_0$, where mv is the mass times the final velocity minus m times the initial velocity. Here we are spared measuring a rate change but retain our attention to the changes occurring after impact. The arguments in favor of applying this concept to impact goes further than the alteration of a formula. Descriptions in terms of vectors (directional measurements) in contrast to scalars (measurement alone)[3] are important in considering the bullet travel.

Inertia   There is another way of looking at impact action. Devices can be designed to detect the magnitude of a beating blow. The devices are called *force tensors,* but what they measure is called *inertia.* This applies Newton's First Law of Motion which states: *a body in uniform motion will remain in uniform motion unless some external force is applied to it.*[9] That is, nothing moves (or changes movement) unless there is a reason for it, and that reason can be treated as a measurable function.

The problem is that the terms and arguments used, are all applied to the same concept in a crime scene context, i.e. blood drops recorded as an impact spatter pattern. Advocates of each formula have good arguments perhaps because under certain circumstances all of them can be applied to blood dynamics. For technical purposes, and research, the formula must be understood. From the analysis of actual crime scenes, which formula is used may seem irrelevant. The important practical issue is how to identify those patterns which have resulted from impact dynamics rather than other acts such as Cast Off and Arterial Damage.

As stated in Chapter 2, class characteristics of all spatter patterns include an exposed blood source which receives an application of some kind of force and results in separated drops being distributed over some kind of flight path. Further division is possible.

CAUSE AND EFFECTS OF IMPACT DYNAMICS

The blood source for impact spatters may exist as prior exposed, as in the case of beatings, or be exposed at the moment of impact, such as with gunshot. The amount of blood available will vary greatly. If the amount of blood varies, the number and size of spatters will also vary. For this reason size and shape of individual spatters alone cannot identify an impact event.

The force applied is an impact, a direct application of an essentially instantaneous event. There is direct contact between an object and a surface (victim or other) with blood inbetween. The degree of contact will be variable, perhaps highly variable. The object used to strike a blood source can be broad/narrow, flat/round, hard/resilient, and short/long. The blood source itself can be rounded/flat, cushioned with hair/muscle/fat/clothing, or on a hard non-absorbent floor/side walk/ground. Contact may be at right angles or slanted through any of 90°.

NON-NEWTONIAN FLUID EFFECT ON IMPACT DYNAMICS

Blood trapped between surfaces will experience shear. Shear (two surfaces sliding in opposite directions), causes turbulence of the flow and may result in drop separation aside from the parameters of impact. The strong cohesion of blood can be seen in a frame from the training film *Blood in Slow Motion* (Figure 3.1).[10]

Figure 3.1

A hammer projects a film of blood which separates after expansion.

AREA OF CONVERGENCE

In Chapter 2 it was shown how spatters can be viewed to determine their Direction of Travel when contact was made with a target surface. In the case of Impact Spatters this technique can be taken farther. Lines are drawn through the axis of each of several spatters and extended back in the direction from which the drop of blood came. If the pattern is the result of a single impact, the lines of spatters from that impact will cross. The lines will not come to a point because no two drops will originate from the same point. Drawing spatter directions of travel to a point for such events as blunt force assault suggests manipulation of the direction of travel lines. It is also a loss of information to do so. The area of convergence represents the two-dimensional size and shape of the origin of an impact. See Figure 3.2 for an example.

RECONSTRUCTION OF THE ORIGIN

The sequence of blows during a beating and differences between entrance and exit wounds with some hand guns may be illustrated with areas of convergence alone. Refer to Figures 3.3 to 3.5. Three homicides occurred in a small residence. An eye witness stated where the victims were when shot with a variety of firearms. In the bedroom two patterns are found, one on the wall under the window and one on the ceiling above and near the window. Measurements would be unreliable with the spatters due to considerable bone, tissue, and spinal fluid in the patterns. The spatters did show directions of travel. Lines

Figure 3.2
An area of convergence
example for impact
spatter.

Figure 3.3
Several spatters with bone,
hair, and spinal fluid are
seen under a window and
on a ceiling in a small
bedroom (not shown).

Figure 3.4

Lines drawn through the spatter directions of travel show an area of convergence under the window. One stain, marked with a dotted line, is out of context.

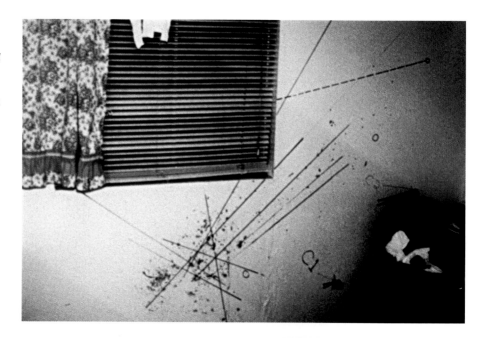

Figure 3.5

A styrofoam ball is positioned at the intersection of two areas of convergence (under the window and on the ceiling). An origin estimate is possible where impact spatters were not measurable.

were drawn through the stains with a felt tip marker. An area of convergence was located on each surface, wall and ceiling. A string was attached to the middle of the ceiling area and dropped to the position of the wall area. A syrofoam ball was attached to the string. One stain was out of context with the rest (shown with a dotted line in Figure 3.4). This spatter was acceptable for measurements. An angle was calculated and a string drawn from the stain along its line of travel to the opposite wall. It passed through the position where the eye witness placed another victim.

Concern has been expressed regarding false areas of convergence.[11] Workshop mock crime scene exercises have shown a greater problem from false points of convergence and points of origin. The first two lines through spatters are done correctly, but subsequent lines are drawn while focusing on the cross of the first two. Students tend to take the term 'Point of Origin' literally. Drawing spatter directions of travel lines beyond their true convergence may create situations of more impacts than actually occurred, and/or extend the event away from the true origin. Constructing a good Area of Convergence is quicker and easier than selecting and measuring Impact Spatters. There tends to be less margin of variation with Areas of Convergence than with individual measurements of spatters. The area of convergence is often more reliable, especially when injury has dispersed bone and tissue with blood. Again, the size and shape of the Area of Convergence can show the size and shape of the origin. It is a waste of information to ignore it. Figures 3.6, 3.7, and 3.8 show differences in Area of Convergence construction on a practice target of known dynamics.

Another way to view impact dynamics is to reconstruct the origin by string reconstruction. Spatters are measured, angles are calculated, and strings are drawn to an area in space where the spatters originated. This is discussed with techniques in Chapter 10. Several computer programs are available to speed up this time-consuming technique. Unfortunately, computer models often omit the Area of Convergence information. Origins calculated are usually called *points of origin*. This should be reported as *a point which lies within the locus of the origin*, since no origin of an impact will actually be a point.

To clarify the relationships: the Areas of Convergence are always on surfaces. This is where the event is recorded. An origin is located in space, where the actual event occurred, at right angles to the Areas of Convergence. For each impact, there is only one origin, but can be two or more Areas of Convergence. When it is necessary to determine where an origin was located at the moment of an impact, it is best to do the work of a reconstruction, string or computer assisted.

Figure 3.6

Practice target is shown of a blunt force impact pattern.

Figure 3.7

Lines are drawn from groups of stains to 'points of convergence'.

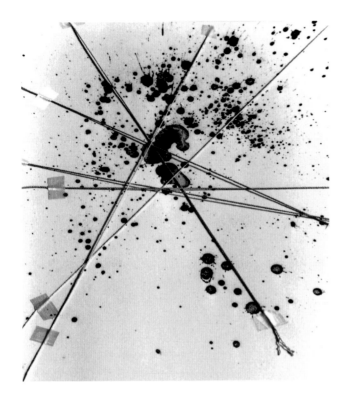

Figure 3.8
*The same target is shown
after drawing widely
separated stains back
without concern for where
they would cross. This
results in a more reliable
Area of Convergence. The
'weapon' for the single
impact was a skillet.*

OBJECTIVE APPROACH APPLIED TO IMPACT PATTERNS

Based on the dynamics of impact, there are criteria which will aid in the identification of Impact Spatter patterns. Key facts are instantaneous contact, considerable variance, and distribution away from an Area of Convergence/Origin. Five criteria can be described for impacts:

Shape of the whole pattern The shape of the whole pattern will reflect an origin and directions of individual stains distributed away from it. Shapes must include those patterns recorded from impacts at various angles. Both Balthazard and Piotrowski considered angles of assault resulting in whole pattern shapes. Descriptions applicable to impact whole patterns include: pie wedge, star burst, sunrise, cone, trapezoid, and folding fan.

Alignment of individual spatters with respect to the whole pattern Lines drawn from the spatter back to the origin will appear as spokes in a wheel, stays in a fan, rays in a star burst, etc. An expression used in reviewed reports and transcripts is *outward in all directions* from the convergence. Refer to Figure 3.9 for examples of individual spatter alignment in the whole pattern.

Alignment of individual spatter stains with respect to each other   Each blood drop distributed from a single impact travels a separate path. No two drops can originate from the same point of the blood source. A possible exception to this is described for *splash*, described later. All blood drops in an impact spatter pattern will be along separate lines drawn from the origin. Each resultant spatter will, therefore, be at some angle to all the other spatters in the pattern.

Figure 3.9

Example of impact spatter distribution.

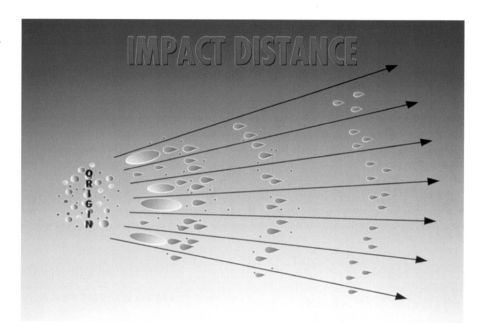

Distribution (or density) of the number of spatters   The blood source provides blood from only one location, with some blood drops deposited all along the path away from the origin. Since some drops are lost from the initial array as a function of distance it can be said that spatter density decreases away from the origin. Two qualifications must be considered: if the impact is a gunshot and/or an object provides blockage. These will be discussed later.

Distribution (or frequency) of spatter size ranges   Because impacts involve considerable variation in the amount of contact and thus force application, different size drops will be distributed. As the pattern proceeds large drops will fall close to the origin because their mass is more quickly overcome by wind sheer. The fact that drops are large suggests insufficient momentum is transferred during the impact. As the distance increases away from the origin, mist is lost because of size. Mist sized drops may dry and be dissipated on air currents before they are recorded on a surface. Fine and small sized blood drops travel a little farther and usually leave stains but are affected by wind sheer. They may settle leaving a round stain, rather than hit a target at an angle. Medium sized stains are capable of traveling farthest from an impact. They have sufficient mass and have received sufficient momentum at impact. Spatter density (distribution) decreases from the origin as well as size ranges. Although string reconstruction and computer approaches are available, investigators do not always take the time and expense to apply them. Approximate size ranges and number of stains at intervals away from an apparent area of convergence can be recorded for future evaluation.

DEFINITION OF SUBGROUPS

Impact dynamics includes several variations in patterns. Each of these have specific characteristics which aid in identification:

Bludgeoning   Beating a victim with an object provides the greatest variance to impact spatter patterns, yet information gleaned can provide extremely probative investigative leads. Caution is suggested in identifying those spatters associated with the actual impacts. Beatings of multiple blows will usually include Cast Offs from the weapon. Directions of Travel will all be away from the origin/convergence of the impact. Areas of Convergence are very helpful in determining possible type of weapon and number of impacts.

If multiple blows strike a blood source, an increase in the number of spatters may be seen as well as an increase in the spatter size ranges and size of Areas of Convergence. These may be used to corroborate Cast Off patterns for estimating the number of blows delivered.

Splash   A common device in training bloodstain pattern evidence involves a spring loaded trap. Blood is added to a flat lip and a pin is pulled. A top flat plate slams shut to project blood drops. The principle is *Splash*, a pool of blood on a flat line receiving an impact from a flat upper plate. Case application for this is a shoe fall into *Volume* blood. The main feature of the pattern is the low angle at which drops are distributed from the origin. The pattern is usually one of streaks and lines associated with volume blood. A shoe fall in a pool of blood or as transfer after stepping in blood is a common example of splash, as shown in Figure 3.10.

Gunshot   See Chapter 9 for a discussion of gunshot dispersed impact spatter.

Exhalation   This term is preferred to others such as inhalation, inspiration, and expiration. Blood drops are projected out rather than taken in as with inhalation and inspiration. Expiring is more commonly interpreted as 'giving

Figure 3.10

A shoe fall example of a splash impact spatter pattern.

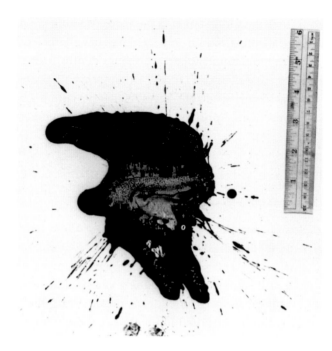

up' as in a victim expiring or time expiring. Exhalation is the act of breathing out which is the dynamics involved. The force causing impact is air from the lungs. The degree of force may be as light as wheezing, (shown in Figure 3.11) or as strong as a sneeze shown in (Figure 3.12). The blood source is positioned in and around the mouth and nose.

Depending on the amount of blood and degree of force, spatter patterns may include a predominance of drop sizes from fine through large. Mucus and cells from saliva may or may not be seen. The whole pattern shape is usually helpful. Cough and sneeze are often round or oval whole patterns. Wheeze is seen as bell shapes. Because the patterns are contained in shapes caused by the nose and mouth, density differences may not be noticed. Patterns are also usually directed at right angles to the target. Spatters are thus recorded as round with little or no direction of travel. If there is a lot of blood present, large drops may be distributed. If there is too much blood in the drop to be contained within the spatter, it will flow toward gravity. This overflow should not be mistaken for direction of travel.

AMYLASE VERSUS PATTERN IDENTIFICATION

Criminalists often favor chemical tests over pattern criteria. Amylase enzyme testing is suggested for blood from the mouth (high amylase levels)[12] versus blood vessels (low amylase levels). There is a practical problem with this logic. Amylase is an inducible enzyme, produced as the response to food and

salivation.[13] That means it is not always present in the same concentrations. Eating, thoughts of food and/or attempts to stimulate saliva will increase the amount of salivary amylase. On the other hand, a person in fear of their life may experience extreme dry mouth with much less amylase present. If blood is copious as from an injury to the mouth, throat, or lungs, exhaled blood may not demonstrate high enough amylase levels to verify exhalation spatters. Urine, pancreatic fluid, and intestinal drainage may also contain elevated amounts of amylase. The rule should be that if the level is very high, and other sources of contamination are eliminated, the blood source was most likely the mouth. If the level is within blood amylase levels, conclusions should be verified by other methods. An excellent alternative is recognition of exhalation bloodstain patterns.

Figure 3.11 (above left)
Two forceful wheezes were directed towards a soft cardboard surface.

Figure 3.12 (above right)
One of two sneezes found at a homicide scene.

CONCLUSIONS

Size of spatters should not be used as the sole or predominant criterion for differentiating impact acts. The distribution and density of size ranges provide more information. Impact patterns must not be identified subjectively from injuries. The same size spatter could occur from other acts. It is far more important to identify the spatter then look for the blood source than to approach the evidence in reverse.

REFERENCES

1.   DiMaio, Vincent J. M. (1999) *Gunshot Wounds Practical Aspects of Firearms, Ballistics, and Forensic Techniques* (2nd edn). CRC, Boca Raton, FL, p. 58.

2.   MacDonell, Herbert Leon and Bialousz, Lorraine Fiske (1971) *Flight Characteristics and Stain Patterns of Human Blood.* US Department of Justice, Washington, DC, p. 20.

3.   Lough, Patricia Schechter (1998) *Impulse and Momentum of Impact Bloodstain Patterns.* Presentation at AAFS 50th Annual Meeting. San Francisco.

4.   Bürkholz, Armin (1989) *Droplet Separation.* Verlagsgesellschaft. Republic of Germany, pp. 1–2.

5.   DiMaio, Vincent J. M. (1999) *Op. cit.*, pp. 58–62.

6.   White, Harvey E. (1962) *Modern College Physics* (4th edn). D. Van Nostrand, Princeton, New Jersey, pp. 114–118.

7.   *Dictionary of Physics* (1977) (ed. Valerie Illingworth) Penguin Group, London, p. 320.

8.   White, Harvey E. (1962) *Op. cit.*, p. 40.

9.   White, Harvey E. (1962) *Op. cit.*, p. 40.

10. *Blood in Slow Motion* (1991) Video. Home Office Main Laboratory. London.

11. Bevel, Tom and Gardner, Ross M. (1997) *Bloodstain Pattern Analysis with an Introduction to Crime Scene Reconstruction.* CRC, Boca Raton, FL, p. 123.

12. Tietz, Norbert W. (Ed.) (1983) *Clinical Guide to Laboratory Tests.* WB Saunders, Philadelphia, p. 54.

13. Moss, Donald W., Henderson, A. Ralph and Kachmar, John F. (1986) Chapter 5, 'Enzymes', in *Textbook of Clinical Chemistry* (Ed. Norbert W. Tietz). WB Saunders, Philadelphia, p. 726.

The Death of Major Person, 6 January 1781 by J.S. Copley,
by permission of The Tate, London 2000.

CHAPTER 4

CAST OFF SPATTER GROUP

The frontispiece (opposite) illustrates blood dripping from a wounded soldier. The drops, however, are illustrated as 'plewds', artist's representations of liquid drops. This artist was known for his accuracy in depicting battle and war scenes. It is this misconception about drop formation that emphasizes a need for clarification for the benefit of average individuals in the jury pool.

CAUSE AND EFFECT OF CAST OFF DYNAMICS

Like all of the spatter groups, Cast Offs result from an application of force to a blood source causing drop separation and distribution. A blood source must be exposed and blood accumulate prior to cast off dynamics. Three possible sources may be exposed:

- Actively bleeding wounds.
- Blood coated weapon.
- Blood accumulation on materials.

Impact spatters essentially result from immediate dynamics at or near blood source exposure. By contrast Cast Offs require a time span before drops separate. This is from the time of blood source exposure to when accumulation is sufficient to coat a transport medium. The medium may be material, fibers, objects, weapons, or other parts of the crime scene. Since cast off dynamics span a range of space, blood drops may be added to the array over the path of travel. This will be seen in a greater uniformity of spatter sizes, i.e. few different sizes in the size range, and distribution of numbers.

After blood is exposed and accumulates, Cast Off force may be applied in two ways:

- Gravitational force pulls downward.
- Centripetal force pulls outward.

GRAVITY, GRAVITATION, GRAVITATIONAL FORCE

Gravity is defined as everything drawn to the earth's center.[1] When attraction is expressed as acceleration, it is referred to as gravitational force. Some of the greatest names in science, Galileo, Newton, and Einstein, have contributed to the modern understanding of gravitation. The gravitational force is a universal law, affecting the behavior of heavenly bodies. The local effect on earth is the pull of gravity downward, acting on the vertical plane only, not horizontal. This confuses some individuals who perceive gravity stopping horizontal motion. What occurs when something falls to earth after an arc flight path involves two forces: gravity pulls down (vertical effect only) and air friction (wind sheer) pushes in reverse (horizontal and/or forward direction). In a vacuum, theoretically, objects fall at the same rate regardless of their mass (density times the volume), although markedly different surface areas will show slight differences in rate of fall. Items of different mass and shape do not fall at the same rate in air[2] due to air friction. Those who continue to argue that gravity can act horizontally should be aware that another term for gravitation is *weight*. It is the gravitational pull vertically that creates the concept of weight.

TERMINAL VELOCITY

Terminal velocity (see Chapter 2), occurs when an equilibrium is reached between gravitational force pulling downward and air resistance pushing upward on a body in vertical fall. If power is continually added to promote horizontal travel, such as a boat traveling through water or an airplane traveling through air, terminal velocity may be reached in which a constant velocity is set on the horizontal plane. With blood drops, after distribution is initiated, no further force is applied and drops will slow from air resistance. How soon they slow will depend on their initial velocity (Paul Kirk's concept of drop velocity rather than force velocity) and their mass (weight divided by volume). The mass is influenced by hematocrit. The volume of drops vary according to injury, material from which drops fall, and conditions of separation.

CENTRIFUGAL VERSUS CENTRIPETAL FORCE

A common misconception is that an angular momentum (spinning in a circle) projects objects outward in curved flight paths. Since the perceived direction is away from the center, it is called *centrifugal force*. Physicists, however, consider centrifugal force fictitious.[3] The opposite force, *centripetal*, is accepted as real. This force acts as a tether holding whatever is spinning to the core. To satisfy Newton's Third Law of *equal and opposite forces*, there must be an opposite to centripetal force. This is centrifugal force, whether considered real or fictitious, and acts to pull spinning objects away from the center.

The main misconception is that objects released from horizontal centripetal motion will follow a curved flight path. The usual analogy is a ball on a string being spun around a center pivot. If the string is abruptly cut, the ball travels a straight line according to the coordinates at the moment the string is cut. Cast off blood drops figuratively behave as balls released from cut strings. The point of cutting the string is analogous to that point in time and space where adhesion of blood to a transport medium (weapon, bloodied material, etc.) is overcome by angular momentum.

NON-NEWTONIAN FLUID BEHAVIOR EFFECTS ON CAST OFFS

The main parameter of cast off drop separation is the adhesion between blood and the transport medium. Adhesion depends upon the nature of blood and properties of the transport in relation to blood. Drop separation is influenced by the non-Newtonian fluid mechanics. The higher the hematocrit, the greater the elasticity of the fluid. High elasticity results in blood elongating rather than separating into a drop.[4]

DROP SEPARATION IN CAST OFF

Drop separation for viscoelastic non-Newtonian fluids involve three events:

- Stretch, a function of the elasticity of the fluid.
- Deformation, the ability and manner of a fluid to respond to stress.
- Separation, an end point to a fluid's ability to compensate under strain.

Viscosity acts with non-Newtonian elasticity to influence how far a fluid will stretch before a drop will separate. Since this depends in part on the hematocrit, and hematocrits vary, drop size for a specific crime situation cannot be standardized. With the same sample of blood, drop size can appear uniform, but the same sample will not exist at crime scenes. The belief of blood uniformity is a fallacy that has existed for some time. An excellent example of stretch may be seen in the British video, *Blood in Slow Motion* (see Figure 3.1)[5] where horse, not human, blood was used. The greater viscoelasticity of horse blood used in filming showed a blood film expanding from an impact by a hammer, before drop separation occurred. Horse blood flows at a higher temperature than human blood. The choice of horse blood was excellent for conditions of filming, however, elasticity (stream elongation) exceeded what would be

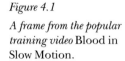

Figure 4.1

A frame from the popular training video Blood in Slow Motion.

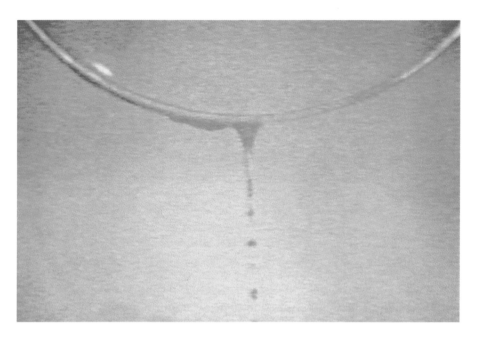

expected from human blood. This was also noticeable in the Drip Cast Off pattern from the plastic Petri dish as seen in Figure 4.1.

Newtonian fluids show truncation, shortening of the fluid behind a forming drop.[6] Inelastic fluids have drop separation from breakage, while non-Newtonian fluids stretch before drops separate. During moving Drip Cast Off exercises in bloodstain pattern workshops a pattern may be seen of a big drop with a smaller falling near. Workshops usually use out-of-date transfusion blood for the exercises. Additives to the units reduce the viscosity for prolonged storage.[7] The small drop/big drop pattern does not relate to normal fresh shed blood unless something is affecting the viscosity.

Behavioral differences can be seen in comparing deformation of Newtonian with non-Newtonian viscoelastic drops (see Figure 4.2).[8]

Cast Off drop separation may occur along lines directly from the source. This permits an arrangement called an *inline* spatter pattern. Impact, by contrast, has drop separation radially. All Impact drops radiate from an origin, thus inline spatters from the same position are not possible. A caution is noted not to confuse secondary spatters of Impact Spatters with inline arrangements. The key to inline pattern identification is that three or more spatters of almost the same size are along the same direction of travel line. Secondary spatters are much smaller and found in front of (in the direction of travel) a *parent* spatter.

A factor in the size and number of blood drops that may be cast off depends upon the nature of blood involved and interaction between blood and the transport medium. Blood is composed of cells and liquid. These interact with a transport media in predictable ways. Properties of the transport medium may be divided into categories: Absorbent, Non-absorbent, and Inert.

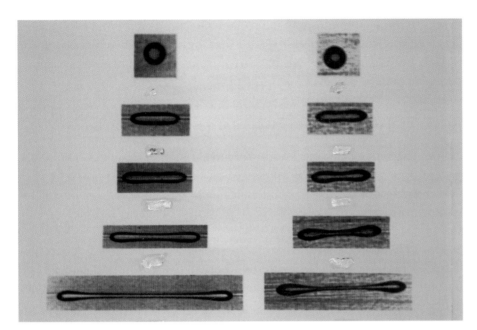

Figure 4.2

A comparison of Newtonian (left column), and non-Newtonian (right column) fluids showing different degrees of deformity during drops responding to stress. Reprinted by permission of Elsevier publishers.

Absorbent transport   Blood readily coats such materials as natural fibers and unfinished (or worn finished) wood. The nature of adherence, however, is not necessarily uniform. Liquid from blood may be absorbed into places along the material but red blood cells are left on the surface, or delayed on the surface until they can migrate or be forced between fibers. This may remove some of the liquid from blood and result in drops concentrated in red cells. Drops cast off such weapons will be smaller and heavier than if the blood is distributed by non-absorbent transport. This situation may explain small and medium sized very dark to tar like stains seen at some beating homicides.

Non-absorbent transport   Some materials, such as iron and steel, do not absorb blood but will have a thin layer bond form on the surface. Less blood will coat the non-absorbent transport than the absorbent one, but the adhesion may appear stronger. Drops require more force to separate from a thin coat on a transport such as metal, than is necessary to dislodge drops from a heavier coated transport such as wood. This occurs because of the thickness of blood layers. A thin layer of blood adheres to the transport material itself, while thicker layers actually adhere to other layers of blood, not directly to the transport. Adhesion between blood coating blood is less strong than blood coating the transport.

Inert   Some materials not only do not absorb blood but do not retain any evidence of blood contact. Teflon is an example as well as are many plastics and waxed material. Vinyl and latex protective gloves repel blood to some extent, although not as efficiently as Teflon. Materials with uneven properties such as wood grains, complex fabric weaves, and uneven finished/painted/worn surfaces will provide whole cast off patterns with greater spatter size variations than for a uniform surface composition.

OBJECTIVE CRITERIA APPLIED TO CAST OFF PATTERNS

Actions distributing cast offs are expressions of motion dynamics. The whole pattern arrangements will be influenced by velocity of motion, whether the motion is linear or angular, the amount of blood involved, and the nature of the transport medium. Objective criteria for all cast off categories include:

Shape of the whole pattern   Cast offs are usually arranged as linear, rectangular, or 'eyebrow' shaped whole patterns. Unusual shaped transport media, large quantities of blood on the transport, and material variations may alter the whole pattern shape (see Figure 4.3).

Figure 4.3

An example of Cast Off eye brow linear whole pattern shape. Note subtle shift in alignment and sizes.

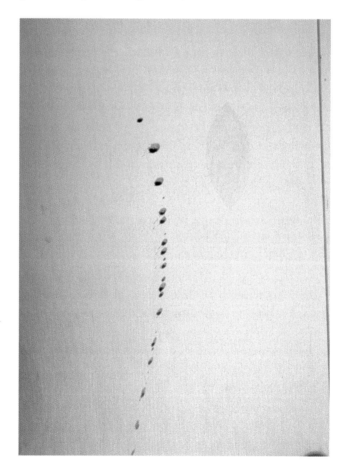

Alignment of spatters within the whole pattern Cast off spatters show direction of travel in line with linear and rectangular whole patterns but may include a series of angular shifts especially in curved or 'eyebrow' whole patterns. This arrangement changes from spatters at an oblique angle through the line of the whole pattern to an in line arrangement.

Alignment of individual spatters with respect to each other Cast Off spatters may be completely in line with each other or as parallel arrangements. Curved arrangements usually show a transition from nearly parallel to each other to a nearly in line arrangement.

Alignment of individual spatters with respect to each other Cast Off spatters are not intentionally measured for reconstruction of an origin because drops distributed by cast off action do not originate from a common origin. The variation in sizes over the range of a whole pattern is useful in a general approach. The number of different sized stains usually remains fairly constant over the range of the pattern. This suggests a uniform consistency to the transport medium. Three or more sizes throughout a pattern suggests uneven motion (jostling, jerking, abrupt changes in direction) and/or multiple transports and/or multiple textures of a transport.

Distribution of number of spatters A time interval with a blood source contributing is suggested when the frequency of spatters remains constant over the range of a cast off pattern. If the number of stains is relatively consistent with an abrupt end, the pattern is more likely to be a Cast Off than an Impact Spatter pattern.

Distribution of number of size ranges The forces involved in Cast Off drop separation are more uniform and predictable than Impacts. Better control and uniformity may have contributed to acceptance of the paddle fan (Cast Off principle) to demonstrate velocity effects on drop size. Although the dynamics are the same, some pattern differences exist in the Cast Off subgroups.

DEFINITION OF CAST OFF VARIATIONS

There are three related actions which distribute Cast Off spatters:

- Dripping, drop separation by gravitation alone (classified as Drip Cast Offs).
- Thrown or flicked, drops separated by centripetal force (classified as Swing Cast Offs).
- Continuing flight after the transport medium stops, momentum transfer (classified as Cessation Cast Offs).

DRIP CAST OFFS

Dripping blood is the simplest form of cast off action. The blood source must be bloody enough to drip, i.e. actively bleeding wounds or wet blood soaked materials. The drops will usually be large. Gravitational force acting on the blood source is relatively uniform. Relative uniformity of drop sizes with subtle size shifts make up the whole pattern. Several different spatter sizes may be found in a Drip Cast Off pattern if jostling, multiple transports, and/or various textures of transport material are involved. Arrangements of spatters are usually linear, but may be broad rectangles or composed of multiple adjacent linear tracks. Inline arrangement is the rule, i.e. a series of stains with the same line Direction of Travel.

The rate of forward movement may affect the shape of Drip Cast Offs. Slow movement leaves round stains, while fast movement yields elliptical ones. The difference in shape is subtle so that speed of the blood source is measured more by spacing of the stains than length of the oval. Blood from a nearly stationary or slow moving object leaves closely spaced, large stains, which may result from multiple drops hitting in tandem (*Blood into Blood*). Irregular motion distributes Cast Offs of variable size. An even flowing wound drips uniformly and abruptly stops. A dripping material, such as clothing, may show gradually wider spaced stains instead of an abrupt stop.

Since drops from Drip Cast Offs are usually large, there is a great deal of edge characteristic variation. Spines, spikes, and scallops are seen. Satellite spatters may occur. As mentioned in Chapter 2, Direction of Travel can be determined as the edge with the greatest irregularities. In the case of Drip Cast Offs that would be the segment of the circumference with the longest spikes and most satellite spatters.

The size of individual spatters in a drip cast off pattern depend more on the nature of the blood source and random movement than on the vertical distance between the blood source and the recording target. Measuring such stains to determine how far the drips fell is not a practical procedure. See Figures 4.4 and 4.5 for examples of Drip Cast Off found at the scenes of assault with knives.

SWING CAST OFFS

Swing Cast Offs result when blood drops are thrown, by *centripetal force*, from a swinging object. Force application is more uniform and distributed over a range of time and space. Considerable size range overlap between Impact Spatters and Cast Offs have been seen in casework, although Cast Offs may include a predominance of larger size ranges than for Impacts. Stains recorded on vertical

Figure 4.4

Drip Cast Offs are seen across a sidewalk at the scene of a knifing assault. Directions of travel are subtle and only determined for a few of the spatters. The general direction is from right to left as viewed.

Figure 4.5

A few cast off patterns were in a 'cane' whole pattern shape. These have been duplicated with flicking actions. The dynamics are a combination of drip and swing.

surfaces may be influenced by gravity, and thus may result in comma shaped spatters if the swing is low velocity.

Swing Cast Offs blood drops will travel along flight paths determined by vectors acting upon the drop at the position and time of drop separation from the transport medium. Distribution is affected by three components: horizontal (side to side, x axis), vertical (up to down, y axis) and horizontal (front to back, z axis). In theory vector analysis is beneficial here. An important observation regarding swing cast offs is that they cannot be used to locate an origin. Not only do drops not have a common origin, they represent different positions of the transport medium over a range of time and space. No common origin is involved. An example of a swing cast off from an injured arm is shown in Figure 4.6.

Figure 4.6

An eyebrow shaped whole pattern with large spatters in an almost perpendicular arrangement shows the arm wound was bleeding freely when moved during standing position.

Six interpretations are important with swing cast offs:

- The minimum number of delivered blows
- Where the reverse in the swing occurs
- Where the ends of the swing occur
- Size and shape of instrument moving/swinging
- How well the instrument being swung holds blood
- Method of swinging the instrument or object used

The minimum blows delivered to the victim will equal the number of swing patterns plus one or more. At least one blow must draw blood, and only those blows which receive sufficient blood will project Swing Cast Off patterns. Several blows are usually involved before blood drops are distributed to form a Swing Cast Off pattern.

Locating the end and reverse of a Swing Cast Off pattern depends upon where the pattern is recorded, which reflects how the swings are performed. Backtracking from Swing Cast Off patterns can suggest how a weapon was used, which is *investigative leads* information.

If a swing is overhand, the stains may be deposited on ceilings, floors, and form perpendicular arrangements on walls. Bloodstains in a linear pattern cascading down the back of a suspect's shirt or jacket are suggestive of involvement in a beating with overhand blows. If the swings are all batters' style, the patterns will be deposited as roughly horizontal arrangements on walls, rarely floors, and not ceilings. Back handed swings, or variations of batters' positions, may have upswing chops at the reverse. Cast Offs may not always be found on the assailant's clothing since the majority of blood drop distribution is away from the weapon, and possibly away from the wielder of the weapon. A significant use from this pattern type is to determine if the weapon was used left or right handed, or even ambidextrous.

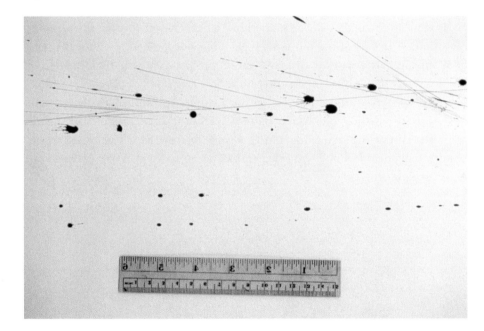

Figure 4.7

An overhand swing is shown with both reverse (away from the blood source) and forward (toward the blood source) indicated.

Sometimes a complete 'V' shaped whole Cast Off pattern is encountered. If the sides of the 'V' have different size ranges of spatters and Directions of Travel, the position of the blood source (victim) can be suggested. The larger stains represent the back swing, while smaller stains represent the forward swing. Larger drops occur when the weapon is the bloodiest, immediately after contact with the blood source, and require less force to be dislodged. Smaller drops require more force to break surface bonding, as they stay on the weapon longer. Greater force occurs from a forward blow to a victim rather than for a reverse swing away from a victim. Therefore, smaller drops show the Direction of Travel toward the victim and bigger drops show the direction of travel away from the victim. See Figure 4.7 for an example of a Swing Cast Off pattern.

Bloodstain pattern workshops have given rise to a misconception regarding cast offs. An assumption may be encountered that blood only comes off on the back swing, i.e. away from the blood source. Cast off exercises in a workshop usually involve giving students a weapon, such as a length of pipe or ball bat, and instructing them to do reverse swings from a blood soaked sponge. The student touches the weapon to blood then flicks it over his or her head. The objective is to create bloodstains, not produce bodily injury. The back swing, away from the bloody sponge, is the most forceful. The return to acquire more blood is less important to the student so is not carried out as forcefully. There is often a snap at the end of the back swing. Being more forceful, the back swing projects more drops than the return swing to the sponge. The end snap is analogous to flicking a towel in locker room play, and clears the weapon of blood. The forward blow to the sponge does not cast off drops.

A crime event makes the forward blow to the blood source/victim more important. The back swing is intended just to position the weapon for the next blow. A snap may not occur, or may occur at the victim instead of at the end of the reverse swing. With weapons that hold only one layer of blood, drops may not be projected until the forceful forward swing. This illustrates the caution necessary in equating bloodstain pattern workshop observations with actual casework. At the end of a swing, either reverse or forward, a part of the whole pattern may include some scattering of individual spatters. These spatters are *Cessation Cast Offs.*

Figure 4.8

A reconstruction with an axe leaves a line of cessation cast offs with distribution from right to left.

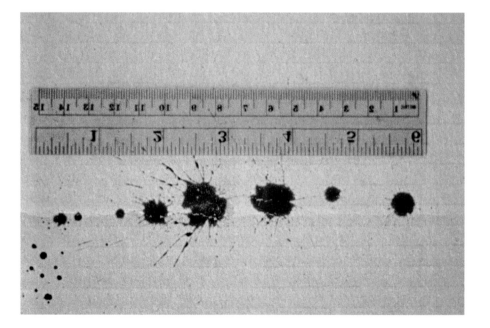

CESSATION CAST OFFS

Cessation Cast Offs occur when a moving bloodied weapon or object immediately stops. The blood drops coating the weapon continue traveling in the same general direction, arrangement, and same relative speed as they were traveling before being dislodged. Refer to Figure 4.8. Drop size is similar to swing cast offs under the same conditions, with perhaps more overall size variation. Spatters will usually be more rounded, which results from drops meeting the target at right angle. Under some conditions cessation cast offs will be projected so that angular, tear drop shaped spatters are recorded. This can be valuable in reconstructing the dynamics of a crime. It is essential, however, that separate acts be recognized.

Defensive gestures of a victim when blows are struck with a bloodied weapon are common examples of Cessation Cast Offs. Whole pattern linear arrangement may identify a narrow weapon such as a knife or axe blade. Broad whole patterns define broader weapons. Exceptions occur when the Cessation Cast Offs are recorded on surfaces at a distance, for example over 2 feet from the blow being struck. The longer drop flight paths may result in divergence, making weapon width estimation unreliable. Variations are encountered with patterns deposited at the end of a swing where spatter closely resembles impact spatters (see Figure 4.9). These may be inadvertently used in reconstructions of the origin. If a string reconstruction is performed correctly, lines will diverge instead of crossing at a common origin. Computer programs may create multiple origins if cessation Cast Off stains are entered into the program. See

Figure 4.9

A five feet tall man was beaten below this 6 feet high rod. Spatters deposited above the rod indicate defensive motions while standing.

Figure 4.10

Three spatters are located on a to scale photograph of a wall at the scene of a homicide. The stains were selected for students to use because they could be measured.

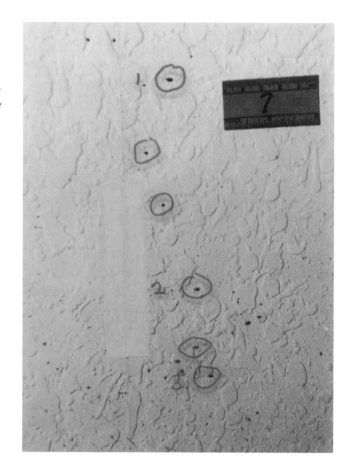

Figure 4.11

Constructing a correct area of convergence shows that the stains are cessation cast offs, not impact spatter. The time to measure and calculate angles is saved. No origin of impact spatters can be determined from cast offs. Three other stains do come to near a point. The assault was with a narrow steel rod. The origin, however, was determined from other evidence to have been near the door jam, right edge of the mounted photograph.

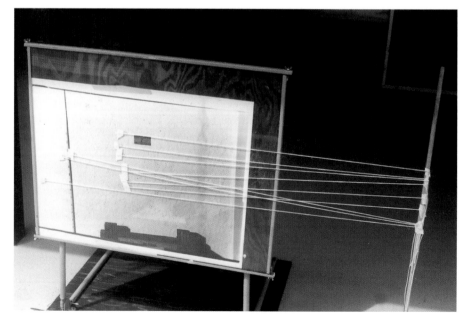

Figures 4.10 and 4.11 for a crime scene example of cessation cast offs originally identified as impact spatters and how a full string reconstruction illustrated correction of identification.

CONCLUSIONS

It is essential to note the important difference between cast offs and impact spatters. No origin location can be concluded with cast off spatters. The patterns, however, can prove valuable in suggesting weapons, bloodied objects, and movement, over the range of time and space during the crime.

REFERENCES

1.   Boger, David V. and Walter, Kenneth (1993) *Rheological Phenomenon in Focus*. Elsevier, Amsterdam, p. 140.

2.   *Concise Encyclopedia of Science and Technology* (4th edn) (1998) (Ed. Sybil P. Parker). McGraw-Hill, NY, p. 907.

3.   White, Harvey E. (1962) *Modern College Physics* (4th edn). D. Van Nostrand, Princeton, New Jersey, p. 31.

4.   *Concise Encyclopedia of Science and Technology* (4th edn) (1998) *Op. cit.*, p. 180.

5.   Boger, David V. and Walter, Kenneth (1993) *Rheological Phenomenon in Focus*. Elsevier, Amsterdam, *Op. cit.*, pp. 130–133.

6.   *Blood in Slow Motion* (Video) (1991) Home Office Main Laboratory, London.

7.   Sears, Francis Weston and Zemansky, Mark W. (1955) *University Physics Complete Edition* (2nd edn). Addison-Wesley, Reading, Massachusetts, p. 229.

8.   Heaton, William and Andrew L. (1986) *Enhancement of Cellular Elements in New Frontiers in Blood Banking*. AABB, Washington DC, p. 105.

A pottery shard displayed in the National Folk Museum in Samarkand, Ubetzistan.

CHAPTER 5

ARTERIAL DAMAGE STAINS

The frontispiece (opposite) shows a pottery shard commemorating a battle during the time of Tamerlane (1336–1405). A warrior face is reproduced with a face decoration suggestive of Arterial Gush. The central area is surrounded by smaller dots and painted in a red ochre pigment. If a warrior cut the throat of an enemy and sustained arterial gush, a pattern like this may have been observed in his face. The design could be copied as a badge of ancient battle.

INTRODUCTION

The previous chapters have concentrated on impact spatters and cast offs. A third spatter group is known as *Arterial Damage* patterns. With other groups little regard is given to which blood vessels provide a blood source, as long as one is available. Arterial Damage patterns, however, are significant because of the injury location. Since this is the responsibility of medical science, physicians must be included in the investigative team. It is incorrect, however, to require identification of arterial injury before identifying the bloodstain pattern. A general policy for forensic pathology is not to mention arterial injury unless it is the cause or manner of death.[a] Experience shows that Arterial Damage patterns are usually identified before an autopsy is performed. This provides immediate information, but the fact that an artery was breached, and its location, must be confirmed by medical practitioner.

[a] Personal conversations with pathologists in the USA, Canada, England, and Australia.

NATURE OF THE BLOOD SOURCE

Arteries are vital blood vessels of the human body. They transport oxygenated blood from the lungs via the heart to all other organs. Veins, by contrast, transfer blood back to the heart and in turn to the lungs to receive oxygen for recycling. Because the transfer away from the heart requires continued pressure, arterial vessel walls must be muscular and thus are thicker than veins. In order to breach arterial walls injury must be more severe and deeper to reach those areas protected by the anatomy of the body. The farther from the heart the vessels are located, the greater the pressure.[1]

In addition to the pressure within arteries, the pumping action of the heart adds rhythmic surges to move blood along vessels away from the heart. This action has been compared to the trace pattern of an electrocardiogram (EKG). An EKG is, however, an indirect method of measuring heart and heart valve function.[2] Indirect methods are necessary since direct, intracatheter measurement (needle placed inside an artery) is a serious and life threatening procedure. Arterial Damage patterns at a crime scene, by contrast, are a direct measure of arterial function. The system is under constant pressure with rhythmic surges provided by the heart. An early example of direct arterial pressure measurement was constructed with a dog's tibial artery breached and allowed to spurt against a rotating paper drum.[3] The tracing closely resembled the pattern being formed by simulation in Figure 5.1. Medical literature establishes a history for arterial damage bloodstain patterns.

Figure 5.1

A water fountain pump is used with latex tubing to demonstrate pressurized blood drop projection similar to arterial damage.

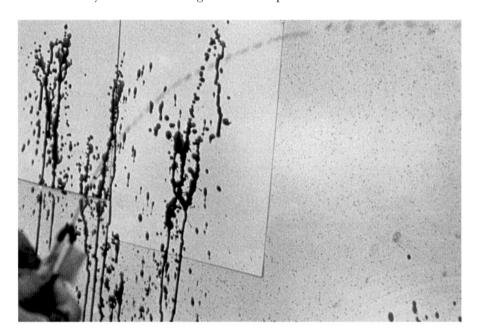

When an artery is breached, blood loss is more rapid than for injuries not involving arteries. This leads to *volume* stains (discussed later) and more serious and immediate damage than if the loss were from comparable veins. Arterial blood carries oxygen, essential for the heart and the brain. With major arterial blood loss, the body immediately reroutes 80% to 90% of the blood flow to the head and heart.[4] The carotids (arteries on sides of the throat which feed the brain) and aorta (main vessel from the heart which follows the spine downward) are critical blood vessels. Loss from these can rapidly lead to death. Locating when and where arterial breach occurred may be essential in reconstructing the events which led to a death investigation.

ACTIONS WHICH PRODUCE ARTERIAL DAMAGE

Arterial injury may result from one or more of three actions:

- Firearms
- Stabbing/Cutting
- Crush/Tearing

Table 5.1 gives examples of arteries which may be breached, location, and type of assault which could cause breach in that area.

Artery	Location	Probable action
Facial	Mouth/lips	Fist, beating, crush
Temporal	Head/temples	Gunshot, crush, (rare stab)
Carotid	Neck, front throat	Knife, gunshot, decapitation
Subclavian	Under collar bone	Gunshot, body crush
Aorta	Chest, upper tummy	Gunshot, stab
Brachial	Arm/elbow	Gunshot, bone break
Radial	Wrist	'Slit wrist', bone break, gunshot (defense wound)
Femoral	Groin	Gunshot, bone crush, stab
Tibial	Ankle	Bone break, crush, firearms
Deltoid	Upper arm muscle	Gunshot, stab/cut

Table 5.1

Areas and actions which may involve arterial damage.

Identifying arterial damage bloodstains requires recognition of body areas where arteries are available for injury. A caution is included regarding the nature of arterial damage. Too often damage is equated with severance, and speculation as to how long after injury a victim could have survived. A mechanism which probably happens more frequently than severance is through an aneurysm. Injury is inflicted on an artery, such as beating. A weakness in the arterial wall occurs producing a bulb extension, like an attached balloon. Subsequent injury may rupture the bulb. This provides a hole breach but may also involve constriction of the arterial vessel. Constriction in the case of some arteries decreases blood loss so that injury need not lead to death, especially if bone and clot material blocks the breach. See Figure 5.2 for an example of temporal artery spurting in a victim who remained conscious and alert, and suffered no permanent injury.

Figure 5.2

Temporal arterial spurting.
Photograph courtesy of Anaheim Police Department.

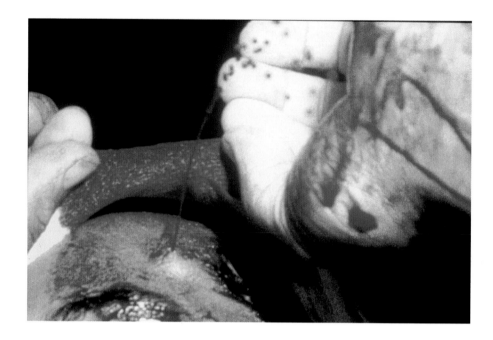

THE NATURE OF THE FORCE

Unlike impact spatters and cast offs, bloodstains resulting from damaged arteries are not dependent upon the criminal acts which precede them. Those stains which are classed as arterial damage patterns, *spurts* and *gushes*, occur as a release of blood under pressure after the fact rather than from a direct assault. Blood drops separate from an arterial stream by rheological dynamics. Once opened, arteries may continue spurting as long as the heart continues to pump and blood is available in the vessel. This means that arterial spurt patterns may be recorded on bystanders responding to the victim after an assailant is gone. Arterial injury may occur without criminal assault. See Figure 5.3 where an alcoholic bled to death after accidental injury to the temporal artery.

NON-NEWTONIAN EFFECTS ON ARTERIAL DAMAGE STREAMING

Streaming is a term used in fluid mechanics to describe flow from a pressurized nozzle. Addition of a small amount of non-Newtonian fluid to a Newtonian fluid may stabilize stream flow, while high value non-Newtonian fluids are noted to be very unstable.[5] This balance between stability and instability with blood influences flow within the body and drop separation following breach. Arterial gush streaming presents a paradox in defining arterial damage dynamics.

A characteristic arterial pattern has been described where a central round stain is surrounded by small satellite spatters. Refer to the Frontispiece for an example. The traditional explanation has been that the satellite spatters result

Figure 5.3

Accidental injury to the temporal artery led to death in an alcoholic victim. Note prolonged arterial spurting behind bed.
Photograph courtesy of San José Police Depart-ment.

from drops of the column striking in tandem. In other words, the small spatters are viewed as ricochet from the main arterial stream. The problem with this explanation is that ricochet should be projected away from the surface, not deposited around the central stain. The pattern for ricochet from the column might show satellite spatters as streaks from low angle projection, but not the dots as seen with some arterial gush patterns.

Rheological studies with streaming fluids illustrates a possible explanation to the satellite spatter pattern.[6] See Figure 5.4 where a stream of Newtonian fluid shows the formation of satellite drops upon forced jet exit of the column. In the body, blood demonstrates both non-Newtonian (red blood cells) and Newtonian (plasma) flow. The speed of the stream may affect stability for both Newtonian and some non-Newtonian fluids. If this is the explanation for an Arterial Gush pattern of a central circle surrounded by satellites, the pattern would be specific for Arterial Damage. Possible theories regarding how the Arterial Gush patterns result include:

- Plasma around the circumference exits with Newtonian behavior.
- Relative velocity of the pressure driven column causes satellite drops to separate.
- Disruption by exiting under pressure destabilizes blood, with satellite separation.

Rheological studies are in progress to evaluate these phenomena.

Figure 5.4

*A comparison is shown
between Newtonian and
non-Newtonian forced jet
streaming.
Reproduced by permission
of Elsevier publishers.*

Newtonian

Non-Newtonian

DIRECTION OF TRAVEL ARTERIAL PHENOMENON

With impact and cast offs the directions of travel are determined by the dynamics of the acts which distribute drops. Arterial Damage has two parameters influencing directions of travel of the drops projected:

- Direction drops projected by arterial pressure.
- Direction victim moves while artery is pulsing.

An interesting phenomenon has been observed both with simulated patterns and in casework. When the victim and the arterial projection is in the same direction, the edge characteristics cancel out, i.e. egg and oval shapes. If the victim moves in the opposite direction to the vessel streaming, the recorded Direction of Travel is accented, i.e. tadpole and tear drop shapes. To use this, the analyst first determines the Direction of Travel, then assigns this to the blood vessel. Next the shapes of spatters are noted and direction assigned to the victim. See Figure 5.5 where an Arterial Spurt pattern is found on a wall between the location of the victim and where the left wrist was likely slashed. The question asked by investigators was 'In which direction did the victim move?' This would relate to where the wrist was cut and to where the victim fled. The body could have been moved afterwards. The direction of travel for the spatters is the direction in which the artery spurted from right to left. The tadpole shapes indicate the victim moved in the opposite direction, left to right.

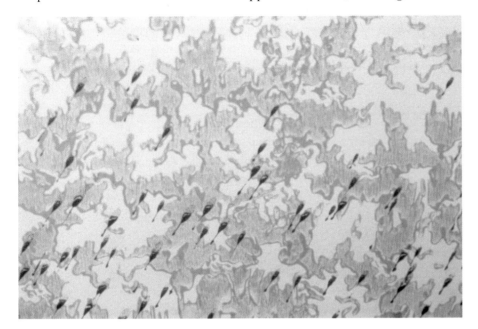

Figure 5.5
Arterial spurt pattern on a bedroom wall.

OBJECTIVE CRITERIA IN ARTERIAL DAMAGE BLOODSTAIN PATTERNS

Compared with Impact and Cast Off, the force involved with Arterial Damage bloodstain patterns is very uniform in nature. This leads to a recurring observation of uniformity of the patterns. Satellite spatters may confuse the inexperienced, but when their nature is understood differentiation is simple. The general criteria are described below.

Shape Shape of the whole pattern usually reflects the undulation of the vessel pressure with 'S', 'V', and 'W' whole pattern shapes possible. Patterns may be broad rectangular, but will usually have one side undulating.

Alignment with respect to whole pattern Individual spatters will align with the whole pattern as parallel rows of stains.

Alignment with respect to each other Here the appearance of uniformity is the most remarkable. Stains will align parallel with Directions of Travel as parallel lines in the same direction. Cast Offs have at times been mistaken for Arterial and vice versa. The key to differentiation is that Cast Off patterns in 'V' arrangements demonstrate two opposing Directions of Travel. With Arterial Spurts it is common to see large ovals on vertical surfaces arranged perpendicular to the floor/ground.

Distribution of size ranges   Again uniformity is the norm. The whole pattern consists of uniform sized stains. If spatters show a shift in angle from the blood source the stains may be shortened or elongated slightly. This will occur as a subtle shift and stains remain in parallel arrangement. In general spatter sizes are large, but high blood pressure from small breach injury may cause separation sufficient to project fine through medium sized drops. In one situation in the author's experience, mist sized spatters were recorded on an assailant's T-shirt from an initial breach wrist artery cut. Because the projection is a forced stream considerable secondary and satellite formation results. These give the overall pattern the look of multiple stain sizes. It must be remembered that secondary and satellite stains are not the primary dynamics.

Distribution of individual stains   Spacing between stains and distributions over the whole pattern continues to demonstrate uniformity. A problem with analyzing crime scene surfaces near where arterial damage occurred is that the volume of blood involved also produces considerable amounts of secondary and satellite spatters. Analysis requires identifying the primary patterns and outlining those spatters from the arterial blood source. All satellites and secondary spatters are ignored. With a major injury and high arterial pressure the pattern may appear to include a wide range of spatter sizes. These are dependent on variations to Arterial Damage.

VARIATIONS OF ARTERIAL DAMAGE PATTERNS

Arterial gush   While the blood pressure is high and/or an injured artery projects in or near one position, the pattern is called a *gush*. The streaming column exits the arterial vessel then separates into drops which hit the target in tandem. The pattern recorded includes a very large central dense circle which is usually surrounded by satellite spatters. The Frontispiece illustrates a decoration suggestive of this pattern type. Sometimes the satellites are deposited as streaks and exclamation marks, or they may be recorded as a row of fine to small sized dots around the circumference of the center stain, as described above (refer to Figure 5.6 for another Gush example).

Arterial spurt   The damaged artery may move so that the separated drops are recorded. This best demonstrates the objective criteria of uniformity. Parallel arrangements of three or more spatters (5–8 spatters improves confidence in

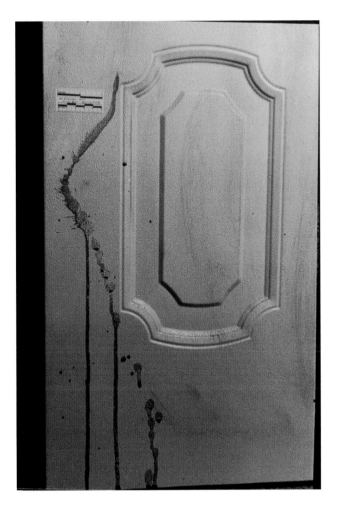

Figure 5.6
An arterial gush pattern from the right carotid artery is recorded on a closet door.

the identification) of the same size and direction of travel suggest an Arterial Spurt pattern. The spatter series may occur close to a small randomly arranged group of spatters. This suggests the site of arterial breach. Without Arterial Spurt, Breach may be indistinguishable from Impact Spatter. When blood pressure drops, the spatters from the Arterial Damage will show effects from gravity.

Arterial spurting along a horizontal path may resemble Swing Cast Offs. In Chapter 4 the formation of a 'V' arrangement was discussed in relation to Swing Cast Offs. The pulsing of arterial pressure can project drops which form 'V' and 'W' shapes. The difference is seen in the consistent directions of travel in one direction only, and parallel arrangement of spatters for Arterial Spurts. Cast Off 'V' arrangements have directions of travel in two directions, and spatters are at slight to marked angles to each other and with respect to the arms of the 'V'.

Arterial fountain   If an artery is aligned vertically with respect to a recording surface, a pattern may be recorded as an indirect fall out of drops. These resemble a water fountain. Parallel arrangement is still present but may include shifts of groups of spatters to resemble cast offs. The key to differentiation is parallel spatters in groups of uniform size and shape. Cast off spatters show some size variation and subtle shifts of angle between adjacent spatters.

Arterial rain   Arterial rain may or may not result from an arterial fountain. In response to pressure decreasing, a projected stream may result in drops falling around a victim. This action resembles rain, and thus the term Arterial Rain has been applied. The pattern appearance is of round stains of varying sizes, predominantly large, and randomly scattered. There is a lack of organized Directions of Travel. Arterial rain patterns are usually identified in combination with other Arterial Damage pattern types. They may be confused with or be a part of Blood into Blood patterns as described in Chapter 9. An example of Arterial Rain may be seen in a shower (Figure 5.7).

Figure 5.7
Arterial rain covers the pan of a shower.

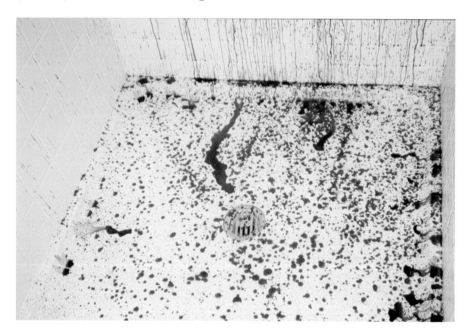

Arterial breach   Breach must be located after other patterns. Arterial spurt and Gush are identified first, then a pattern resembling Impact (if available) is considered as a possible beginning of arterial damage. Streaming (recorded as Arterial Gush), if it precedes drop separation, confirms an Arterial Breach did occur. Breach may follow an Impact event with or without Impact Spatters being seen. It is not correct to identify Arterial Breach simply because arterial injury is suspected. It must be noted that arterial damage can project blood great distances. Figure 5.8 shows the results of decapitation. The two carotid arteries projected blood which was visible from aerial photographs. The 'W' shape was actually caused by arterial gushes from both carotid arteries in two separated positions. Figure 5.9 shows an arrangement of large ovals of uniform size arranged parallel to each other, located between the legs of the 'W'. This recorded how the body pivoted between the major Arterial Gushes.

Figure 5.8
Arterial Gush from both carotids seen in an aerial view.

Figure 5.9
A closer view of Figure 5.8 shows the Arterial Spurt pattern between the legs of the 'W'.

CONCLUSIONS

Because the walls of healthy arteries are thick and muscular, the force necessary to breach them must be greater than that for damaging a vein. Glancing blows with a blunt weapon, shallow penetration with a knife, and the common falls, spills, and tumbles of daily accidents are insufficient to result in arterial damage. This is also due to the body's construction to protect vital parts. To breach an artery it requires a bullet, sufficient length blade knife, strong wielder of a blunt weapon, or a compound fracture from bone injury (as in vehicular assault) to breach, tear, or puncture an artery. In child and elderly abuse, arterial damage cannot be attributed to the normal falls characteristic of these groups.

With smaller arterial vessels, a victim may live for a period of time after arterial breach. Survival of a victim depends on the size of the vessel breached, how long the bleeding proceeds, presence or absence of arterial constriction (and/or blockage), if the vessel was severed or merely punctured, and if transfusion occurs before irreparable damage is done to the brain and/or heart. While the heart pumps, victims may move or be moved with the artery still spurting and/or gushing, even if comatose or technically 'brain dead'. Patterns will be recorded on the walls, floor, furniture, victim, assailant, and uninvolved individuals coming to the victim's assistance later.

Occasionally students will encounter comments regarding *nonarterial pressurized blood vessels*. No bloodstain evidence at crime scenes is projected by nonarterial blood vessels. Major veins, such as the jugular, contains a large cross-section volume of blood at rapid flow. If injured, blood from the jugular will pool faster than from other venous injuries. Pressure from veins, however, is derived from factors within a closed system, not from measurable direct rheological pressure. Flow is pulled toward the heart. When injured, blood volume spreads outwards and slows, causing immediate loss of technical pressure. The formula which governs this principle is:

$$P_1 v_1 = P_2 v_2$$

That is, the pressure multiplied times the flow velocity of fluid on one side of a vessel wall must be equal to the pressure multiplied times the flow velocity on the other side. When the fluid is no longer contained within a vessel, pressure diminishes since velocity is equalized. This holds true for gases and liquids. The patterns called 'pressurized' may result from other dynamics or from unidentified arteries.

A final comment regarding arterial damage stains. The pigment in blood picks up oxygen from the lungs, turning bright red (pigment + oxygen = bright red). The pigment turns bluish red, purple, deep burgundy, or black when oxygen is depleted. As blood pools, stains are exposed to air, and oxygen may be given up with color change over time. Drying slows but may not entirely stop this process. This can create confusion with photographed arterial damage bloodstains if compiled over several days rather than one session.

SOLUTION TO QUESTION IN FIGURE 2.5

The spatters shown in Figure 2.5 are: top, swing cast off; middle, gunshot impact; bottom, simulated arterial spurt.

REFERENCES

1. Geddes, L.A. (1970) *The Direct and Indirect Measurement of Blood Pressure.* Year Book Medical Publishers, Chicago, p. 125.

2. *Ibid*, p. 1.

3. *Ibid*, p. 18.

4. Sohmer, Paul R. (1979) *Hemotherapy in Trauma and Surgery. A Technical Workshop.* AABB, Washington, DC, p. 2.

5. Walters, Kenneth (1993) *Rheometry.* Chapman and Hall, London, p. 238.

6. Boger, David V., and Walters, Kenneth (1993) *Rheological Phenomena in Focus.* Elsevier, Amsterdam, p. 138.

Aboriginal blockage painting thought to be Neolithic era graffiti, Australia.

CHAPTER 6

TRANSFER BLOODSTAIN PATTERNS

The frontispiece (opposite) demonstrates the pattern type of blockage used in Aboriginal art in Australia.[a] The painting has been placed in the Neolithic era of around 12 000 years ago. Guides showing the grounds to visitors claim that the prints were ancient forms of graffiti.

[a]Photograph by Sgt Warren Day, New South Wales PD CID Retired.

INTRODUCTION TO THE NONSPATTER GROUPS

In contrast to the Spatter Groups, Nonspatter Groups have little in common beyond being bloodstain patterns. The group divisions are based on individual group composition rather than related dynamic events. As the title suggests the connecting criterion is that spatters are not essential to identification. Spatter group events, however, may occur after the physiological change and be included in the final composition. The most important observation with Nonspatter Groups is that they represent time and sequence relationships. These may provide individualizing features for investigative leads. Although the term nonspatter may be new to some, the groups of patterns classified under the heading have been recognized for some time.

DIVISIONS OF NONSPATTER GROUPS

Three categories are included within the division:

- Transfers
- PABS (Physiologically Altered Blood Stains)
- Volume

TRANSFER BLOODSTAIN PATTERNS

Individualization features   Spatter groups were described as being *class characteristics*, which means the patterns can be found in different situations and are not exclusive to specific evidence. On the other hand, *Transfer* patterns may lead to the identity of evidence which link a victim, assailant, and materials within a single context. It may be a serious lost of information to concentrate on spatter patterns. Transfer bloodstain patterns may be divided into two subgroups:

- Blockage: Indirect pattern transfer.
- Contact: Evidence in contact with a surface.

BLOCKAGE TRANSFER PATTERNS

Although the term 'void' has been suggested for blockage type patterns, it is not favored here. A void in older lexicon denotes *devoid of matter*, as a void in space. Newer usage equates voiding with emptying out, as voiding a specimen for clinical analysis. The term does not discriminate between Blockage and Absence of spatters other than Blockage. To avoid confusion the terms Blockage and Absence are used here. Blockage patterns result from blocking an array of spatters distributed from any dynamic act, usually Impact, Arterial Gush, and/or Blood into Blood (discussed in Chapter 9). An outline identifying the object which blocked distribution of the spatters may be seen in some situations. Absence patterns, by contrast, result from spatter flight paths not leading to the target, with no actual blockage involved. Absence and void may be interchanged, but blockage is not synonymous with void.

Blockage Transfers differ from other *trace evidence* by not requiring contact between an obstruction and a recording target surface. Although trace evidence may involve situations, such as hair, dust, pollen, etc. carried on air currents without direct contact between target and source, *contact* is usually accepted as equivalent to *transfer* evidence. By contrast, *Blockage* patterns result when blood drops are blocked by an object, thus prevented from reaching a recording surface. The obstruction may touch the target or be positioned anywhere between it and the blood source. This leaves an outline which may identify an object present during a spattering event. Identifying the object and its movement may provide valuable investigative information.

There are two types of Blockage patterns:

- Shadow
- Template

Schematic illustrations of these are shown in Figure 6.1.

A misconception occasionally occurs regarding the size of a blockage pattern and the presence of spatters within the obstruction outline. Violent crimes are very dynamic scenes. The victim and assailant frequently move, often rapidly. This means that a Blockage in one position may not also be a blockage when movement occurs. There will be a decrease of spatters within the blockage

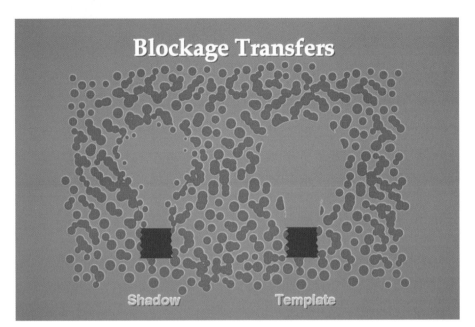

Figure 6.1

Two types of patterns result from an obstruction blocking an array of distributed drops.

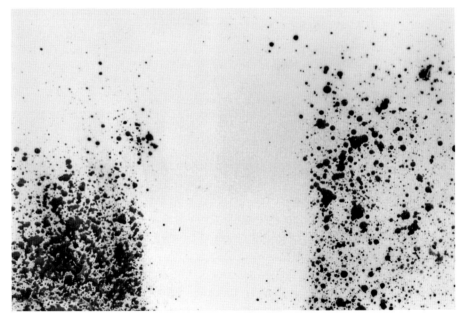

Figure 6.2

Note different densities to spatters on each side of the mug. The impact came from the left as viewed, not at a right angle. The mug was placed 3 inches from the target. No movement was involved other than the simulated impact. Some spatters reached areas within the blockage.

area but not a total absence. Situations of this nature are referred to as *shadowing*, where lighter density of spatter is seen on the edges. Figure 6.2 shows a pattern made by placing a coffee mug between a spattering event and a cardboard target. Round surfaces may permit shadowing by deflecting some spatters touching the object edges. Blood follows the path of least resistance as shown in Figure 6.3.

If the obstruction is close to the target surface, and the spattering event is at

Figure 6.3

Blood follows the curved line of a glass stirring rod rather than straight down by gravitation.

(or near) right angles, the pattern may appear stenciled. The obstruction acts as a template to block completely all spatters from the target. This is referred to as a *template blockage* pattern. The outline should be a representation of the actual size of the obstruction.

A factor influencing blockage patterns is the spatial relationship between blood source, obstruction, and target. Blockage spatial alignment may be used to confirm other determinations of the origin, such as *string reconstruction*, computer location programs, and Areas of Convergence.

An important factor in blockage pattern formation is the distance between the obstruction and the target. If the distance is near contact, the pattern becomes a *template* transfer. This is size relevant and measurements may be used to identify the primary obstruction. Caution, however, must be taken even in this situation. The transfer pattern from a neolithic cave wall shown in the Frontispiece appears to be a template blockage transfer. The distortions of the fingers and the boomerang, however, suggest that the outlining pigment came from an angle other than 90°. The distance between hand and rock could have been near or in contact but the dimensions do not directly relate to the obstructions.

Blockage patterns with spatter on both sides show spatter density heaviest closer to the blood source. The lighter the outline, the farther away it was from the blood source. This same visual analysis can be applied vertically. If the bottom of an obstruction is clearly outlined on a wall or other vertical target, but the top is less clear, the spatter array came from near the bottom or below the level of the bottom. If the top of an obstruction is outlined but the base is not, the spatter array was projected from the level or above the top. Examining the inside of obstructions such as cups, glasses, planters, drawers, etc. will help align the source of spatters. If Impact Spatters are outlining Blockage patterns, these may help locate the origin. When a conclusion regarding the location of an origin is confirmed by two or three different approaches it makes the complete reconstruction conclusions stronger.

Blockage patterns have provided many uses in crime scene investigation. Figure 6.4 shows a victim with Blockage Transfer evidence on her clothes. The assailant claimed the victim was standing at the moment of a shot. Folds in her pants clearly indicate that she was in a seated position. Another example is shown in Figure 6.5. A man claimed to have been assaulted with a knife. All injuries were sustained on the left side. The victim was right handed. He admitted to leaving the hand print on the fireplace. Note the blockage of all but the fingertips.

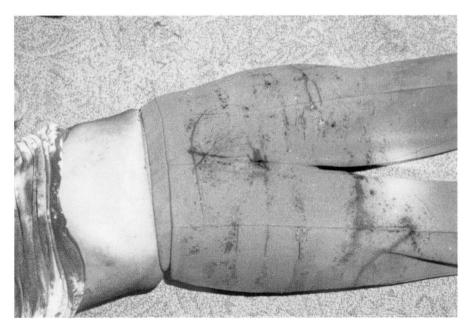

Figure 6.4

Folds in the victim's pants show that she was not standing when the spatters were deposited.

Figure 6.5

Hand print of alleged victim (right handed) of knifing attack (all to the left side).
Photograph courtesy of Roseville Police Department.

CONTACT TRANSFER PATTERNS

Transfer patterns also result from contact between surfaces, one or both bloodied. This pattern type may be included with normal contact trace evidence evaluation. Appearances of such patterns are influenced by: the type of action which transfers blood, the condition of surfaces involved, the material texture and characteristics, and PABS (Physiologically Altered Blood Stains) involvement. All of these conditions affect patterns, which means working in reverse can help determine what occurred and in what sequence. Because contact bloodstains are often *individualizing* (unique), they can be the most important case evidence collected.

Each of the above conditions contains variables which may be encountered with crime scene investigation.

TYPES OF ACTION

There are three combinations to be considered.

- *Simple Direct Transfer* (touch contact without movement).
- Motion of one surface against a stationary surface.
- Motion of both contacting surfaces.

CONDITION OF BLOODIED SURFACES

- Moving surface bloodied and stationary 'clean'.
- Moving surface 'clean' and stationary bloodied.
- Both surfaces bloodied prior to contact.

There are several possible *material texture characteristics.* Although this might seem endless, the important criterion can be broken down into pairs of characteristics which have distinct effects on the results of transfer:

- Absorbent versus nonabsorbent (sometimes called porous versus nonporous).
- Rough versus smooth.
- Distinctive weave or relief design versus no weave or relief design.
- Water repellent and/or chemically treated surfaces versus worn surfaces or no treatment.

In addition PABS (*Physiologically Altered Blood Stains*) involvement will affect the final bloodstain appearance. The conditions of PABS to be considered include:

- Partial or complete drying of bloodstains before contact.
- Contact transfering blood from a *Volume* (pool) of settled blood.
- Contact involving blood where clotting has initiated.
- Fluids other than blood also involved in the transfer.

Although these criteria appear numerous, some either cannot occur or have never been identified as significant in investigation. Refer to Chapter 7 for information regarding PABS.

SIMPLE DIRECT TRANSFER

As the name suggests, this pattern involves a direct contact between surfaces. Blood is transferred directly between surfaces during contact. Surfaces may transfer or receive transfer unevenly. Fresh, liquid blood can be absorbed by a material on contact. Some material, such as unfinished wood, knit fabrics, laminant wallpaper, textured walls, and carpets absorb the stain unevenly. The results may be distortions of the transfer compared with the original. Fortunately one or more dimensions of a distorted transfer will usually be reliable. See Figure 6.6 for a simple direct transfer of a knife used in a homicide. The bedspread was folded over the blade producing two side images. Using the scale photographed with the transfer pattern, investigators were able to match a weapon, found with the assailant, to the crime scene.

Figure 6.6

A simple direct contact transfer resulted from the assailant wiping a knife blade on a bedspread after using it in a double homicide.
Photograph courtesy of Queensland Police Department.

Figure 6.7

The transfer of the knife was found alongside the victim. For a right-handed assailant, straddling the victim is indicated when the knife was wiped.

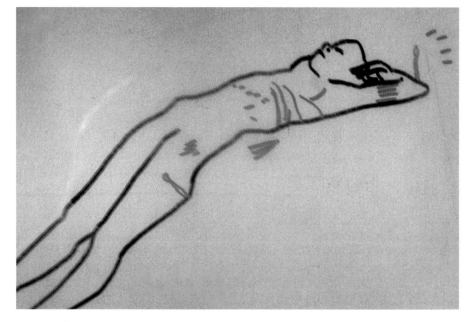

Another variation of simple direct transfers involves blood viscosity. A volume blood pool on a nonabsorbent surface has adhesion.[1] A smooth soled shoe may make contact with the pool, forcing fluid away from beneath the sole. When the shoe is lifted, a vacuum forms. Fluid rushes from the blood sealed edges toward the center to fill the vacuum. The shoe, however, is lifted off before blood can fill the space beneath the sole. Where migration stops, a pattern of concentrated red cells is left. The appearance varies, but may

Figure 6.8

A steam iron has left bloodstain transfer which not only identifies the iron, but also shows how it was handled. The red cells are pulled as the iron lifts off: right edge first, left edge second, and base last.

resemble beading or short streaks. This process can be demonstrated with any flat surface. See Figures 6.7 and 6.8 for examples from different positions and lift off of a steam iron.

Simple Direct Transfers in sequence can be used to suggest how a bloodied object was handled. Figure 6.9 shows transfer patterns on a carpet which appear as smudges until observed at closer contact. In Figure 6.10, the sequence of stains suggest that a hammer bounced, making contact with different positions

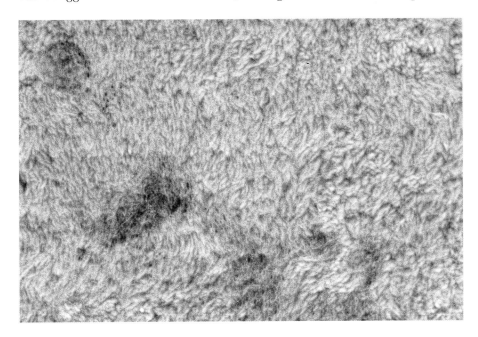

Figure 6.9

A series of transfer patterns are seen on a carpet near a wall.

Figure 6.10

Outlines and shadow sketches are used to illustrate the parts of the hammer recorded in the transfers.

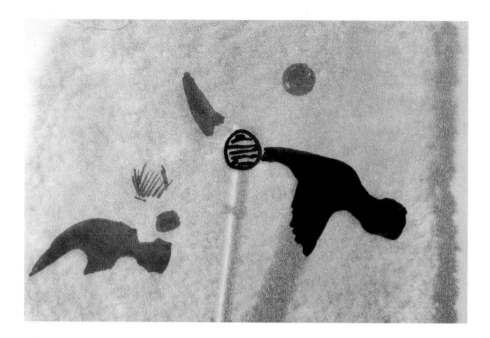

Figure 6.11

The hammer bouncing is positioned to reconstruct sequence during criminal events

on the hammer head before coming to rest. Figure 6.11 shows the transfer sequence in relation to a wall.

PINCH TRANSFER

A pattern often encountered involves transfer during an effort to grasp clothing when the hands are bloodied. This may occur with assailants attempting to move the victim. It may also result when coroners or paramedics collect bodies for transport. The transfer involves gathering the clothes so that two or three areas are pinched together. The result is a three cornered arrangement of large irregular patches (Figure 6.12).

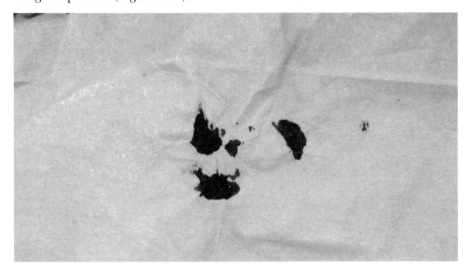

Figure 6.12

A three cornered pinch stain is seen on a sheet used to transport a body.

MOVING TRANSFER, ONE MOVING SURFACE

Bloodstains which result from one surface moving against a stationary surface have been defined on the basis of which is bloodied. Each of the moving patterns shows depths of pigment from red cells (Figure 6.13). Red blood cell concentration is used to determine both direction of travel and type of action. It may be important to identify which surfaces were bloodied and in which sequence during the events of a crime. The actions are labeled:

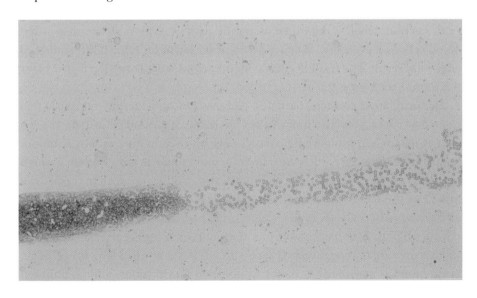

Figure 6.13

Visual perception of moving transfer blood-stains is based on the density of red cells.

WIPE

[b]Terminology of the International Association of Bloodstain Pattern Analysts.

A *wipe* pattern occurs when a nonbloodied surface moves through/across a stationary one.[b] In this action, blood is deposited along the path of movement, increasing in stain depth as it progresses. When the motion ceases with lift off, a sharply defined, denser stained edge results. (see Figure 6.14).[2]

Figure 6.14

A wipe pattern is demonstrated by blood on a surface being moved along by a nonbloodied cloth. At lift off the stain is concentrated in red blood cells. Reproduced by permission of ACPR, formerly National Police Research Unit Reviews of Australia.

SWIPE

A *swipe* pattern occurs when a bloodied surface rubs across a nonbloodied one. In this action, blood is deposited along the path of motion, decreasing in red blood cells as it proceeds. When movement ceases, at lift off, a faint 'feathered edge' may result. The leading edge at lift off provides the Direction of Travel for the action (see Figure 6.15).

Because blood contains particles, patterns not only identify materials that came into contact but also how contact was made. Wipe and swipe patterns can be useful in determining what materials were involved in the transfer. A smooth regular moving surface will leave a smooth, more uniform pattern than a rough irregular one. Cloth folds, nonabsorbence, and wadding are seen in the pattern as well as the fact that surfaces were bloodied. Cleaning a weapon can leave identifying patterns as to its size, shape, and characteristics. An absorbent wipe removes blood. A nonabsorbent one does not. Skin wiping over a bloodstain yields a smooth, homogeneous (evenly spread) pattern with a dark lift-off edge, as no blood is absorbed. A glazed or polished fabric (satin, taffeta, polished

Figure 6.15

A swipe pattern is demon-strated by drawing a natural hair wig across the target from left to right.
Reproduced by permission of ACPR, formerly National Police Research Unit Reviews of Australia.

cotton, chemically treated) will produce a relatively smooth wipe or swipe pattern but with a lighter leading edge than for a skin wipe, because some blood is absorbed by fabric. Although generalizations may be made, it is always advisable to study fabric/material behavior with blood before drawing case conclusions.

MOTION STAINS, BOTH SURFACES BLOODIED

Rarely a combination of actions may occur in which a swipe and wipe overlap. If the surfaces are different, such as hair swipe and cloth wipe, it may be possible to recognize the actions involved. If both surfaces are bloodied and beginning and lift off do not overlap, edges may be identifed.

Occasionally the investigator encounters obvious contact stains which cannot be classified as Simple Direct Transfers (physical match) or moving contact (Wipes or Swipes). These may result from both surfaces being too bloody, movement in two or more directions (such as attempts to clean up the scene), or distortion from very absorbent material. The safest way to classify such patterns are as *smudge*, stains too distorted to classify regarding their mode of production or Directions of Travel. Caution is also noted in interpreting wipe and swipe patterns during bloodstain pattern workshops. Students often reconstruct a wipe pattern but move the transfer beyond the point which would end a wipe, i.e. the action becomes a swipe.

Special cases arise when the wiping surface is damp. Blood carried along with the wiping action in contact with water will hemolyze blood. See Chapter 7 for PABS/mix details. In brief, the action destroys the ability of the red cell to retain pigment. Water soluble pigment is released along the path of the wipe. This action produces a smoother, lighter pattern with quicker diffusion into absorbent materials.

Hair leaves distinctive patterns both at Simple Direct Contact and in Swipes. One result of contact is the pattern called *inline beading*. When blood coats a normal hair strand, it does not adhere evenly. Instead, natural oils cause 'beading' and spotting along the shaft as shown in Figure 6.16. The beaded pattern is transferred to a target surface. The phenomenon is usually not seen with synthetic fiber or old wigs where natural oils have been lost. Body, facial, and scalp hair can all transfer this type of pattern. Wipes and swipes with hair show individual strands as well as locks in the patterns. It is important to note where the blood sources exist in proximity to hair in order to provide a potential for transfers. (See Figure 6.17.)

Figure 6.16

A microscopic view shows blood coating a human hair with one bead formed.

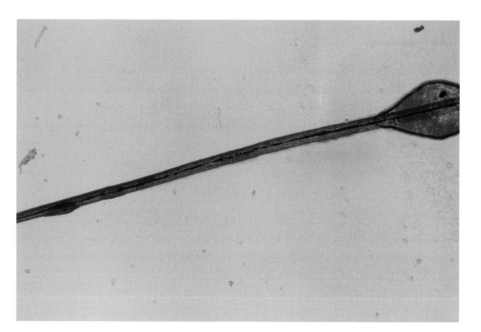

Three PABS patterns are worthy of comment in regard to contact stains: drying, clotting, and mixing with water. The first two provide excellent time indicators, and the third provides conditions of the scene. Blood spattered on a surface will begin to dry immediately. The thinner parts will dry first, and thicker areas last. Wiping with a dry material will remove only the wet part of the stain. Finding wipe marks over a completely or partially dry bloodstain indicates both the relative sequence of events and a time lapse in between. Note that the exact amount of time for a bloodstain to dry involves several variables which

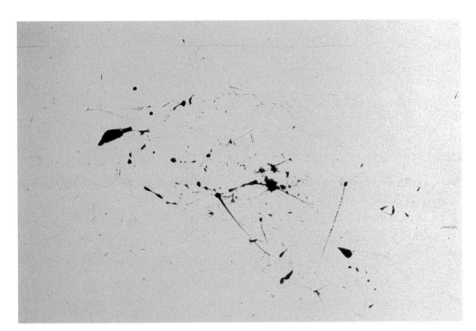

Figure 6.17

A victim of an assault to the face fell against a door. Blood on the hair does not mean injury to the head. Conclusions are that blood reached the hair prior to the stain.

must be considered before drawing conclusions with crime scene evidence.

Clotting blood shrinks as the clot proceeds. Cloth or paper products which acquire large clot fragments may contract with the blood. This indicates that clotting was not finished when picked up by the material. Coagulation and blood mixes prior to contact with cloth are discussed in Chapter 7.

Occasionally a question is asked regarding which side of the material blood made contact. Since the stain may be absorbed, close examination is necessary. Red blood cells are not absorbed by nor can they diffuse through fibers. Gaps in the weave are required for cells carrying red pigment to migrate or be forced. A lighter side to a stain may be seen where some fibers or weave are 'over' the stain. This is the opposite side to contact with blood. Blood cells trapped in the fabric will remain for years and usually continue to give a positive test for hemoglobin.

INVESTIGATIVE TRANSFER

Investigators are often reluctant to discuss situations where either first line officers or part of the investigative team have left patterns in blood at the crime scene. Shoe prints are the most common but examples of protective glove transfer are not unusual, as shown in Figure 6.18. To ignore these in reporting bloodstains at the crime scene is not advisable. It is better to understand and acknowledge their position within the crime scene sequence of events. It is better still to make their occurrence, and the need to avoid them, part of basic training. The label of *investigative transfer* has been suggested to differentiate transfers left by investigative personnel from other transfer evidence. *Contamination* is retained for transfer patterns created by individuals between the completion of the crime and initiation of investigative procedures.

Figure 6.18
The inside of a victim's jacket is shown. The glove pattern was matched to coroner's officers. Note also pinch stains on the garment.

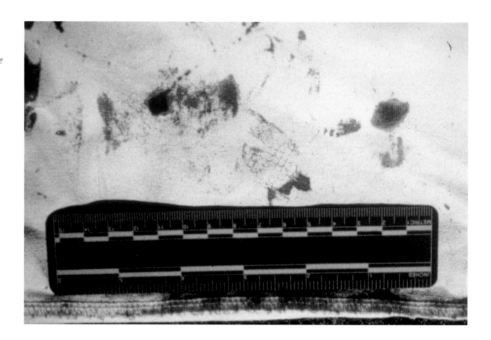

CONCLUSIONS

The importance of transfer patterns cannot be overemphasized. New students of Blood Dynamics tend to focus on the possibilities for spatter group applications at crime scenes. It may be considered that transfer patterns are obvious and already well known. Because blood is involved in the process, however, the interpretation of this group may continue to provide more information than is presently utilized.

REFERENCES

1.   Bevel, Tom and Gardner, Ross M. (1997) *Bloodstain Pattern Analysis with an Introduction to Crime Scene Reconstruction.* CRC, Boca Raton, FL, pp. 57–58.

2.   Wonder, Anita Y. (1987) *Bloodstain Interpretation: An Introduction to the Five Stain Classifications.* NPRU **3**(1), pp. 80–86.

An artist's rendering[a] *of an American Indian medicine man removing a 'snake' (clot material) from a wound*[1] *(16th-century practice in California).*

CHAPTER 7

PHYSIOLOGICALLY ALTERED BLOOD STAINS

Physiologically altered blood stains are those patterns which result when biological changes occur before blood is distributed by other events. The pattern category recognizes that physiological changes to blood may be of greater significance in interpretation than other dynamic acts which may follow. Scientific principles involved in the biological alteration of blood are still being studied, and research will continue to provide information relative to pattern variations. Most important perhaps is that the pattern group provides immediate reconstructive suggestions for investigative leads regarding time lapse and sequence of criminal events.

[a]Sketch provided by artist Jennifer Johnson, Auburn, California.

Four changes are possible after blood is shed:

- Cells may settle.
- Blood dries.
- Blood undergoes coagulation.
- Blood may mix with other fluids and/or materials.

Since these occur under identifiable conditions over predictable sequences and time periods, they provide valuable information for reconstructing events involving blood.

PABS/SETTLED

Sedimentation of blood was discussed in Chapter 1. Only one case has been encountered by the author in which settling was recognized in the evidence. Although the situation and material was identified, the pattern provided no significant information for the investigation. Identification guidelines are presented here for academic purposes relative to future casework.

From the perspective of a crime scene, settling requires two factors: sufficient volume of blood and conditions which result in blood cells sedimenting before drying or clotting occur. As a rule, blood will clot or dry long before red cells settle noticeably. The exact volume necessary depends upon the surface on which blood is found and the depth. Sedimentation will not be identified if blood seeps into fabric such as clothing, carpets, hair or fur. The depth necessary has not been determined but can be as little as a single drop if a highly elevated sedimentation rate exists, and the drop is not flattened.

Three conditions will permit red cells to settle before the volume blood can dry or clot:

- Person on anticoagulant therapy.
- Person has a health condition which accelerates sedimentation.
- Person has defective or depleted clotting factors.

Anticoagulant medication may, or may not, delay clotting long enough for blood cells to settle in a pool of blood. If this situation were encountered in a crime scene context the main questions should be directed to medical physicians regarding the type and effectiveness of anticoagulation. Persons who have lost large amounts of blood with or without transfusion may show delay in clotting sufficient to permit settling. The most common crime scene situation where clotting factors could be defective involves alcoholics. Since these individuals are susceptible to viral infections, a condition which speeds sedimentation, settling of red cells may be encountered at scenes of their injury.

The case involving settled blood viewed by the author involved a young woman who had a recent history of a summer cold. She sustained stab wounds to the heart and bled for a period on a rest-room floor. She revived and fled with a final assault resulting in death in an office area. A lump of white, opaque, sticky gelatin-like material was adhering to her blouse. Infections may increase the clinical sedimentation rate,[2] and apparently affect sedimentation in crime scene blood. Although noted, the pattern type was not seen as significant and not included in a report.

IDENTIFICATION OF PABS/SETTLED

If sedimentation occurs there is a separation of red opaque viscous fluid and clear/colorless to cream/white thinner fluid overlaying. Disturbing the pool may show that the red cells have not clotted. Unless there is sufficient anticoagulant present to prevent all clotting (as with blood used in bloodstain pattern workshops) some coagulation will occur after blood cells have settled. This will be viewed as a layer of clear to cream colored sticky gelatin material. It may adhere to clothing without red pigment being apparent. Testing the material for cellular antigens will be unsuccessful. On the other hand indirect tests may identify serum reverse blood types. DNA tests would be less successful since cellular material may not be present in the clotted upper layer.

PABS/DRY

EFFECT OF VOLUME AND TEMPERATURE

The speed of drying in general depends on three conditions: the volume of blood involved; the temperature of the surrounding environment, and the presence, or absence, of air currents. In the case of spatters, drying is rapid. In fact, observations have shown mist sized spatters from firearms exercises may dry and dissipate in hot, dry, windy areas, leaving no evidence of their presence. On the other hand, deep pools of blood in still air may *crust over*, and not dry for days at cool temperatures. An apparently dry *volume* blood stain on a carpet must be treated cautiously. Seepage under the carpet will remain wet and may not be visible from the carpet surface. This situation often results in investigative transfer.

The most common use of PABS/dry patterns is with flows. Blood seepage will seek the lowest level but also travel along curves according to the path of least resistance. Changing the position of the victim may be seen by noticing flows that have dried. In Figure 7.1 a victim was seen talking to the assailant outside in evening shadows. He became angry but fell as if from drunkenness. The assailant was seen to leave. The next morning the body was found. The question was asked, whether he was knifed in his side before or after he fell. Flow down his side was noted with several secondary flows curving toward his back. These matched pools on the wooden walk where he was found. The victim was upright when stabbed in the side. He fell and did not get up from that position.

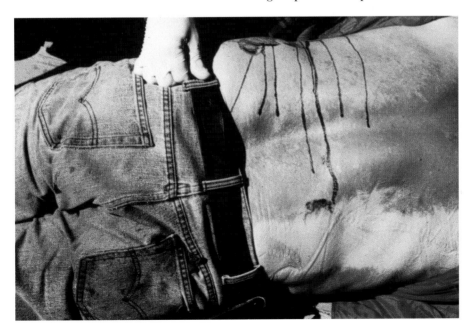

Figure 7.1

An example of PABS/dry suggests that the victim was upright then fell while blood flowed. The assailant claimed victim was knifed while sleeping.

EFFECT OF CLOTTING ON DRYING

If clotting occurs, drying is more rapid than without clotting. Red cells can retain their integrity with clotting and with drying, but are disrupted by combinations of the two. In a crime scene, there may be advantages to collecting an aliquot of liquid blood, where red cell integrity is preserved, before permitting the whole stain to dry.[b] Dried anticoagulated blood will be hygroscopic, since anticoagulation usually involves complexing, or chelating, of calcium. Dried, clotted blood will generally be insoluble in water. Bloodstain pattern workshops often include experimentation with drying using anticoagulated blood. While this is an excellent illustration for students, it should not be directly equated to crime scene evidence. Where drying time is stated in casework, fresh drawn samples without anticoagulation is preferred for interpretation of limits under substantially similar conditions to the crime alleged.

[b]This should be discussed with the relevant crime laboratory for proper protocol.

PABS/CLOT

Coagulation, the ability to clot, is a unique function of blood. Technically the process is complex and continues to be studied in medical science.[3] Although investigators need not understand the full complexity of the process, they should be able to identify clot stage and material as it applies to the reconstruction of crime events. Identification requires some understanding of the principles involved.

PURPOSE AND PROCESS

The main functions of coagulation is to provide a plug at the site of a wound, prevent blood loss, seal the breach from infection, and provide a skin bridge until healing occurs. Unlike drying, the rate of clotting does not depend on the volume of blood nor, from the view of crime scene evidence, within *reasonable limits* of temperature. Clotting does depend on numerous pathological and clinical characteristics of injury. With a *medically normal* blood source and sufficient accumulation of blood that drying does not occur first, clotting will proceed at a predictable rate through three stages. The times provided are approximate:

    Clot Initiation, 2–10 minutes
    Clot Firming, 10–60 minutes
    Clot Retraction, 1–5 hours

Medically normal values are time ranges which have been established for hospitals and clinics over a large number of samples. Time lines for coagulation stages taken from clinical normal ranges do not necessarily apply to crime scenes. When applying these to casework, variation from clinical normal provided by crime events must be understood.

CLOT INITIATION

Two pathways have traditionally been described for initiating what is referred to as the *coagulation cascade*: the extrinsic pathway and the intrinsic pathway.[4] The extrinsic pathway involves injury and applies to forensic investigations, while the intrinsic applies to conditions within the blood and clinical applications. What initiation does is to begin the process where a soluble, liquid, biochemical (fibrinogen) is changed into an insoluble network of sticky threads (fibrin). Injury causes this change to begin. Trauma, compressing and tearing of skin, not only initiates coagulation but hastens it, while clean cuts from razor blades, scalpel, glass fragments, small bullet wounds, and needle tracks may involve less tissue damage and involve longer initiation times. Instant rapid loss of blood such as arterial damage will take longer to initiate clotting. Cold temperatures will delay initiation, while body temperature enhances coagulation.

Clinical data applied to initiation has caused confusion since 10 seconds has been suggested as the time for initiation to take place. This is not untrue, but is irrelevant to crime scene evidence. Coagulation studies in a clinical laboratory use instrumentation to detect different stages of the coagulation cascade. The times within a few to several seconds are characteristic of test results on separated plasma, but not on samples of whole blood from trauma induced wounds. Also, clinical instrumentation is not only unavailable, but would be useless at crime scenes and in crime laboratories.

The clinical test closest to crime scene coagulation is the *Lee White* clotting time. In this procedure, three test tubes, numbered in sequence, receive freshly drawn blood. At intervals one tube is tilted until clotting is noted. Afterwards a second tube is tilted and a third if necessary.[5] Theoretically the two tubes are left to clot without disruption while the first is watched. In practice by the time the first tube shows clot initiation, the other two tubes have already clotted. The method has been discontinued, yet clinical literature often ignores why the test failed to provide a reliable time for external coagulation. Disturbing the clot in tube one prolonged clot initiation, while tubes two and three clotted undisturbed, i.e. movement increases clot initiation time. In a crime scene situation, clot will be prolonged if a continued assault, active bleeding, or vigorous moving of the victim occurs. Although trauma should speed up clot initiation, continually disturbing the clot will prolong it more. Bloodstain pattern workshop times are also of doubtful use in a crime scene context because trauma is not involved. Surfaces upon which blood clots also greatly influence times.

As initiation progresses it will reach that point when red cells become attached to the network in clumps or beads. Drawing a rough, natural wooden applicator stick through the pool will pick up the clumps and strands of the sticky threads (see Figure 7.2). At this stage blood is still more liquid than solid. Visual examination alone will not identify initiation. Impacts, Cast Offs, Arterial Damage, and Transfers involving fragments of clot initiated material can be identified from strands with beading clumps of red blood cells attached. Large stains on fabric may be seen with dark centers and lighter rings (see Figure 7.3).

Figure 7.2

Clot initiation is seen as clumps of material attached to the wooden stick. The blood from which this came did not appear clotted.

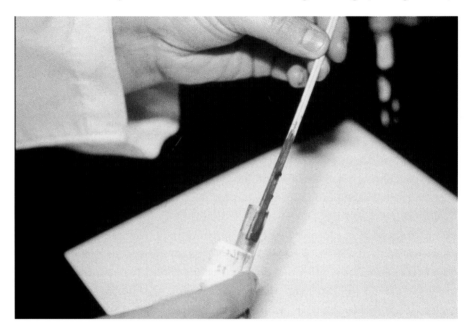

CLOT FIRMING

The stage of clot firming follows *after clot initiation* has spread throughout the sample of blood, provided drying has not occurred. By this time the sticky network has attracted all cells, trapping them in a gelatinous lump. Blood appears *jelled*. Any movement breaks up soft clot fragments with some liquid and a few free red cells. Stains have dark, irregular centers surrounded by paler, pink, area. The stain may resemble a bull's eye. The degree of clot firming may be seen in photographs as the amount of shade change in the outer ring. The closer the shading is to the material beneath the stain, the more advanced is the clot firming stage. Figure 7.3 shows clot firmed material on the inside surface of a night gown. At this stage it is possible to cut the blood pool into pieces as the clot is becoming solid. Undisturbed firmed clot will still resemble fresh blood. There will still be some plasma under the clotting cascade. If the pool lies on a glass or polished surface, attempts to cut the clot will instead move it aside. A pinkish residue, called residual plasma with red cells, will mark the path of the moving clot. The degree of firming can be noted by the lightness of the residue.

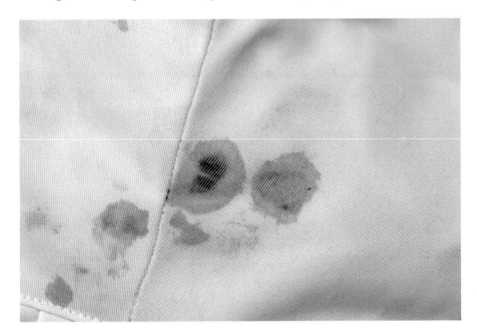

Figure 7.3
A firming clot stain is seen on the inside of a nightgown.

CLOT RETRACTION

Retraction occurs after the clot is firmed. The lump containing all the cells begins to shrink. The cellular mass pushes out a clear thinner liquid from the clot. Pigments in the liquid, which is now called serum, may change to yellow upon exposure to light. Deep yellow colored serum may be found in victims of liver disease such as chronic alcoholics and drug addicts, and those individuals having hepatitis. Serum is less viscous than whole blood, and being Newtonian has less internal cohesion. Serum around a clot on a slight incline will flow away from the retracting clot. The outline of the clot represents the area of the initial blood volume, while the perimeter of the serum flowing around the clot does not. Clot material may not be apparent from a direct lighted view, as shown in Figure 7.4. Examining surfaces with oblique lighting can show the three-dimensional nature of clot fragments, as well as shiny spatters of serum (see Figure 7.5).

Clot retraction can be recognized without the use of wooden sticks or glass rods. The two separate layers are visible. Retraction cannot occur without clot initiation and firming. If blood has not clotted, as with alcoholics, drug addicts,

Figure 7.4

Blood clotted for 150 minutes then was subjected to a spring trap impact.

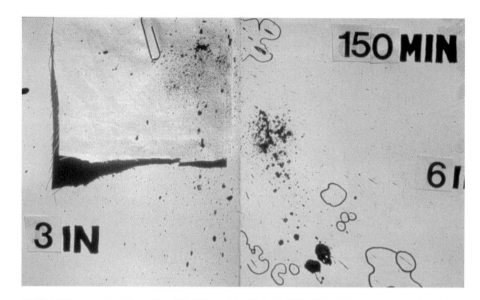

Figure 7.5

The serum stains are not visible from a direct light view. When retraction begins blood behaves as a solid and a liquid.

victims on anticoagulant therapy (so called *blood thinners*), or victims experiencing massive bleeding, clot retraction will not be seen. Clot retraction reported in short time intervals probably represents PABS/settled rather than true clot retraction.

CONCLUSIONS

It is surprising how often clot evidence enters into case work. This has caused some concern amongst scientists who prefer set times for each stage. The dynamics of a crime scene will affect any time ranges provided. The stages can be identified. Exact times cannot be provided to encompass all types of bloodshed. Often a statement is desired regarding how long an assault could have progressed with the recording of advanced clotting (completed firming or retracted). The main condition of any time estimate must be that the assault stopped long enough for clotting to occur. Continued assault prevents normal clotting. If an assailant stops the assault, allowing clotting to occur, then repeats the assault, it will be possible to find advanced clot fragments on the assailant. The sequence, however, increases the time required for the assailant to remain at the scene.

APPLICATION OF PABS CLOT PATTERN INFORMATION

There are at least four uses for clot pattern identification in bloodstain interpretation:

- Time sequence
- Index of contamination
- Impression record
- Degree of force necessary to disperse clot material

Clotting blood is like a ticking clock. After initiation, the changes are steady, predictable, and independent of quantity of blood present over a reasonable range of temperatures, providing that blood does not dry. Events that occur at different stages mark the crime scene with distinctive patterns. The semisolid state receives impressions. The amount of force necessary to propel fragments from stages of clot increases markedly with degree of clotting. Fragments projected distances of several feet require force in the range of gunshot or sneeze. See Figure 7.6 for a clot fragment projected by sneeze.

PABS/MIX

In addition to drying and clotting, blood may be altered by mixing with other materials at the crime scene. The types of mixtures which may be encountered are divided into two groups, physiological (body fluids) and nonphysiological. Examples of each type are:

Physiological fluids
Watery physiological
Cerebral Spinal Fluid (CSF)
Urine

Figure 7.6

A sneeze pattern was found to the right of a window. A single fragment of clot was on the window shade.

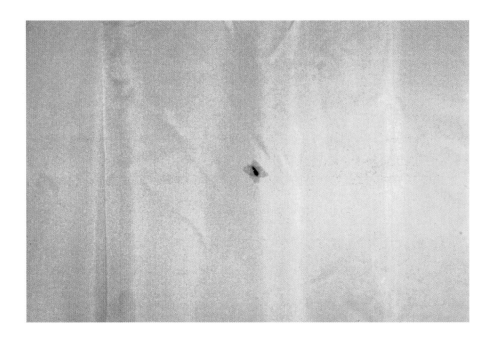

Tears
Middle ear fluid
Some joint fluid

Viscous (mucoid) physiological
Saliva
Nasal drainage
Semen
Vaginal fluid
Rectal drainage
Most joint and serous fluids
Blood (from another source)
Serum

Miscellaneous physiological
Tissue, muscle fibers, organ fragments
Bone and teeth particles
Feces (bowel contents)
Vomit and gastric (stomach) contents
Hair, finger and toe nail fragments

Nonphysiological
Water
Tap, washer, garden hose, bath tub/shower/sink/toilet; drinks (beer, wine,

cocktail, soda, coffee/teas, seltzer, waters); aqueous solutions (liquid soap/detergent, disinfectant chemicals; radiator, clutch, and brake fluid; window (windshield) washer, dew fall, melted snow/ice, river/lake/stream/ocean, aquariums.

Miscellaneous
Flyspeck
Oil, paint, grease
Dirt, dust, ceiling texture, cat litter, metal filings
Fibers

PABS/MIX INTERACTIONS

Three interactions may result from blood mixing with other fluid/materials:

Type 1 Mixture: Blood intermingles but is not diluted.
Type 2 Mixture: Blood is diluted but not changed.
Type 3 Mixture: Blood is diluted and physiologically changed during dilution.

The first listed interaction is seen in blood mixed with saliva, semen, vaginal fluids, and other viscous substances. Both blood and mucoid material retain their separate integrity but are found together. Use of low magnification, hand held or a dissecting microscope, may show clumps of red cells, among strands of mucus. Laboratory techniques are available to separate these (see Figure 7.7).

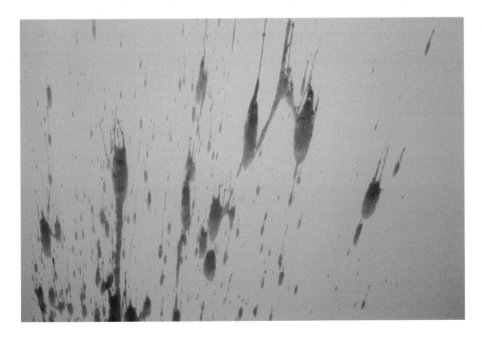

Figure 7.7

A mixture of blood and semen is subjected to a spring trap impact. Note mucoid material with blood.

Blood which is diluted but in which the cells remain unchanged is seen when blood mixes with body fluids such as cerebral spinal fluid (CSF), urine and tears, and other fluids such as salt water and milk. The stains are evenly pink or beige rather than red, rust, or brown. Dried stains have grainy centers which appear opaque when photographed with oblique lighting. See Figures 7.8 and 7.9 for examples of CSF and blood mix patterns. A CSF and blood patterns was found on a wall at the victim's residence. The victim's body was found 5 miles away. The patterns were identified then confirmed by the autopsy pathologist. Blunt force trauma had increased the spinal fluid pressure so that fluid exited forcefully when one blow caved in the skull, X-ray shown in Figure 7.10.

The third type of interaction is blood mixing with water and watery fluids. Water becomes involved when a fight causes drinks to spill on bloodied clothing; an event occurs in the rain, dew, fog, or on a watered lawn; a body is near water, wet ground/floor, punctured water bed; or an attempt was made to wash away bloodstains.

Red blood cells contain red pigment which gives blood the red color. Each red cell is composed of a membrane, called a stroma, which contains the

Figure 7.8 (below left)

A small spatter pattern is found on a wall at the scene of homicide by blunt force trauma. One blow to the head of the victim caved the skull into the area where CSF is contained in the brain. The trauma of beating increased cerebral pressure to 'mist' the pattern on the wall.

Figure 7.9 (below right)

A pink impact spatter pattern is found on the knee area of the pants of the assailant.

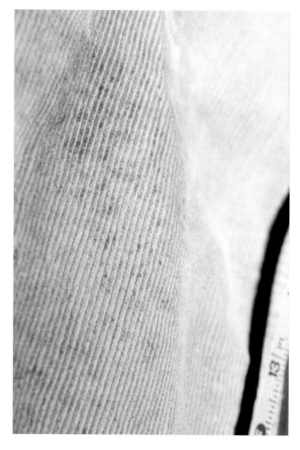

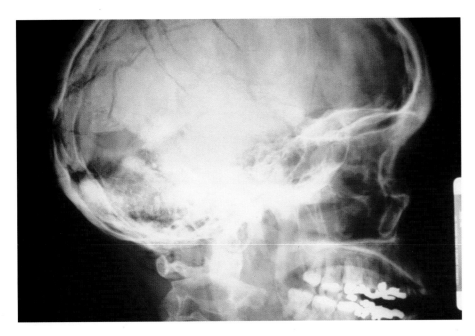

Figure 7.10

The skull X-ray shows an indentation from blunt force which opened the area of the brain where CSF is produced.

pigment. The membrane stability is dependent upon the salt concentrations in the fluids on each side of it. If the red cell is exposed to less saltiness than the fluid within, it takes up liquid. If the outside fluid is water, the membrane takes up liquid until it swells beyond its ability to stretch. This reaction results in cell rupture and the release of pigment, a condition called *hemolysis.*

A stain from blood diluted with water frequently has the appearance of a light beige/buff center with a noticeably darker brown outer edge. Light

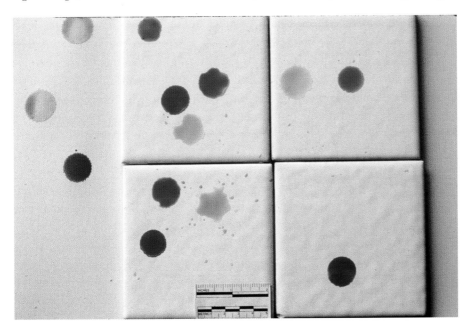

Figure 7.11

Four wet drops are placed on a ceramic tile. Some stains appear diluted but the diluent is not readily apparent. One drop is undiluted blood; one diluted 1:1 with water; one diluted 1:1 with physiological saline; and one is diluted 1:9 with water. Top center tile.

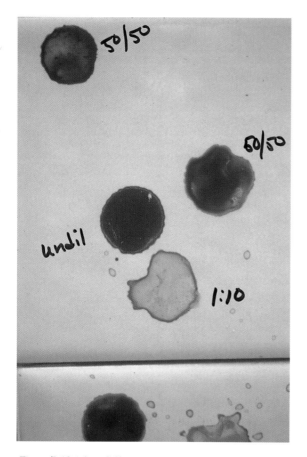

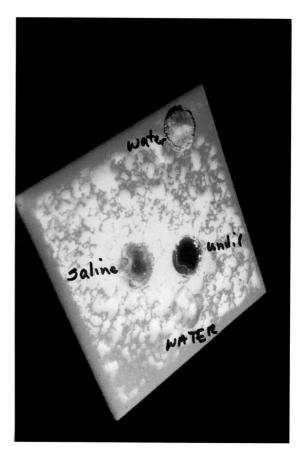

Figure 7.12 (above left)

After the spots are dry the diluted stains are more apparent, yet the diluent is still not known with direct lighting.

Figure 7.13 (above right)

With oblique lighting the differences between the drops is demonstrated. Saline does not destroy the red cell integrity so that the stain is 'dusty' like the undiluted stain. Water diluted stains are translucent showing the sheen of the title under the stain. Observations are enhanced with photographs.

reflected off stains of hemolyzed blood show a translucent center, from the surface under the stain being clearly visible. Examination of stains which appear diluted should always be made with an oblique light after they are completely dry. Type 3 stains may be expected in kitchens and bathrooms where water is available, but should still be distinguished from Type 1 and 2 mixtures. No biochemical test can differentiate blood diluted with water from blood diluted with CSF. Pattern interpretation offers the best approach to identification. See Figures 7.11, 7.12, and 7.13 for comparisons of Type 2 and 3 PABS/mix stains.

BLOOD ON WET FABRIC

Since blood on clothes and other fabrics may provide essential links between victim, assailant, and a crime scene, results of observations will be of benefit to investigators. When blood touches or is dropped on fabric it is not instantly absorbed, since the red blood cells cannot migrate through fibers. Plasma may diffuse but cells must first deform and then flow around fibers. If, instead of dry fabric, blood drops fall onto damp or wet material, the red cells are hemolyzed and red pigment diffuses rapidly. Stains are lighter, larger, and more irregular than if the cloth were dry initially. If the cloth is dry and the blood dries completely before being exposed to water, the stains are much more difficult to wash out. Prolonged soaking will leach red pigment but may leave the stroma, red cell protein coats, in the weave. If this occurs, a paradox may result. That part of the fabric which is red will test positive for hemoglobin but be negative for human cell antigens, while the clear area will test negative for hemoglobin but may provide ABO phenotypes with indirect cell technique (see Figure 7.14).

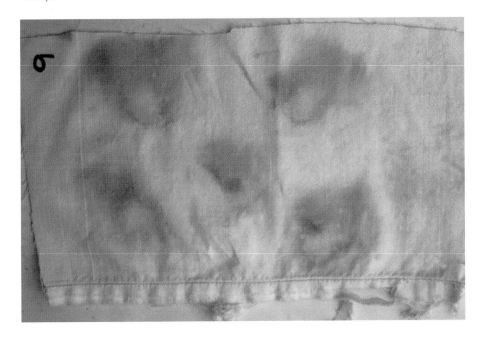

Figure 7.14
A strip of white muslin sheet received several drip cast offs. They were allowed to dry completely. The material was soaked overnight and gently agitated in water at room temperature.

MISCELLANEOUS MIXTURES

In the category of miscellaneous mixtures is a group known as *flyspeck bloodspatter*. Actually bloodstains produced by flies do not result from 'specking', i.e. fly defecation. The actual process is more important than specking would be. After a fly siphons blood, it must regurgitate its own body fluid to equalize aerodynamic balance for flight. Regurgitation returns some blood from the fly proboscis (mouth) mixed with varying amounts of digestive fluid. These stains resemble spatters but include greater variance of shapes, colors, and sizes which are collectively identified as *flyspeck bloodspatter*. The expectorated fluid contains blood which has not been digested, thus may give positive human blood reactions.

If the fly regurgitates and moves aside, a *comma* shaped stain is left. If movement is directly backwards with a large portion of fly saliva, a beige *pear* shape results. If regurgitation is explosive, when flies are disturbed while feeding, the spatter is red to black in color in small round spheres of various sizes. Fly defecation is very small, uniform in size and uniformly beige in color. Eggs may be found, especially on stored bloodstained material. These are uniform tiny white to off-white ovals. An important identifying criterion is that fly material does not demonstrate direction of travel. See Figure 7.15 and 7.16 for examples of fly distributed bloodstains.

Figure 7.15

All the stains shown were deposited by flies over a 24-hour period.

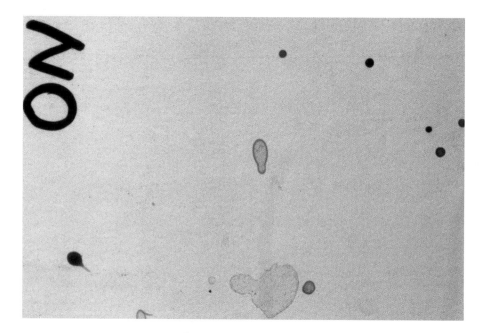

PABS CONCLUSIONS

The patterns included in PABS are not new. New information may be available because research is ongoing in such fields as coagulation. Too often, however, the pattern types are ignored in favor of more familiar subjects such as the spatter groups. If PABS pattern types are given full group status they are less likely to be forgotten during evaluations of crime scene evidence. Unfortunately, much of the information from PABS requires awareness of the potentials before a crime scene is processed.

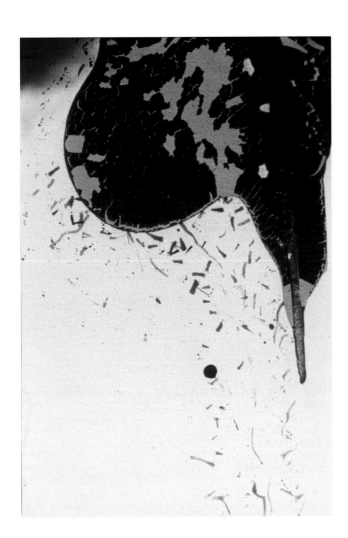

Figure 7.16
The results of a single fly within 2 hours.

REFERENCES

1. Harris, Henry (1932) *California's Medical Story.* J.W. Stacey, San Francisco, p. 7.

2. Tietz, Norbert W. (1983) *Clinical Guide to Laboratory Test.* W.B. Saunders, Philadelphia, p. 177.

3. Dailey, John F. (1998) *Blood.* Medical Consulting Group, Arlington, Massachusetts, pp. 196–198.

4. *Ibid*, pp. 191–208.

5. Mandel, Emanuel E. (1966) *Laboratory Diagnosis of Hemorrhagic Disorders in Todd-Sanford Clinical Diagnoses by Laboratory Methods* (Ed. Israel Davidsohn and Benjamin Wells). W.B. Saunders, Philadelphia, pp. 346–347.

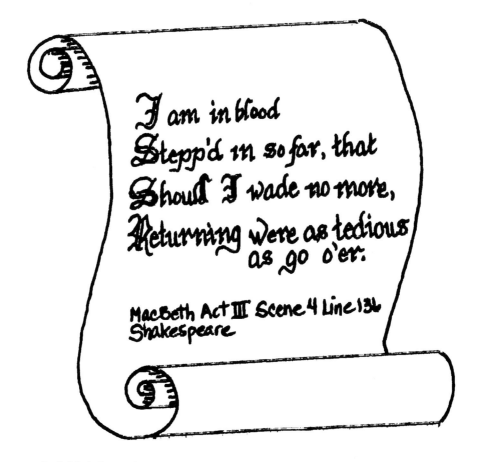

Lady Macbeth monologue by Shakespeare suggests 16th-century volume blood symbolism.

CHAPTER 8

VOLUME BLOODSTAINS

The frontispiece (opposite) gives a quote from Shakespeare.[a] The use of blood and blood volume to symbolize murder and guilt indicates that audiences in the late 16th century associated blood with crime. Lady Macbeth sees this as her guilt in addition to having spatters, spots, upon her person.

Investigators recognize volume blood stains without special training. Other authors have also presented techniques with cautions regarding application.[1, 2] Variations are included here as a pattern category and the significance with respect to other patterns. All liquid pools found at scenes of violence are not necessarily blood. Visual characteristics (red color, viscous nature), behavior (depressions, rings, and flakes with drying) and smell influence identification. Combinations of blood may occur with household liquids, automotive fluids, and water in the crime scene context. The significance of volume blood evidence is often overlooked in favor of other pattern types, yet additional information is available with the pattern classification.

Large volume stains are often encountered before drying is complete. In addition to PABS/clot, PABS/drying, and Investigative Transfer concerns, it may be possible to obtain a preliminary identification of the fluid. For blood the process of drying shows a change from shiny and highly reflective, freshly shed, to a nonreflective patina. Oils do not fully dry, retaining shine well beyond the time for a bloodstain to dry. Aqueous fluids dry leaving no shine or patina.

METHODS OF ESTIMATING

What is contained in a Volume stain has not been formally defined, but can loosely be stated as more than would appear to have occurred from a single drop or even a few drops. In practice what is significant depends a great deal on the individual case parameters. There are at least four approaches for estimating the amount of blood in a pool, none of which is recommended by the author. They are presented here for academic purposes only.

[a]Macbeth, John Bartlett quoted in 15th and 125th Anniversary Ed Bartletts Familiar Quotations (ed Emily Morison Beck), Little Brown and Co., Boston, p. 239:3.

- Plane geometry
- Counting grid squares
- Photographic weight
- Blood dry weight

Plane geometry Plane geometry is used to describe the whole pattern in terms of a combination of geometrical shapes, i.e. circle, oval, triangle, rectangle, or square (see Figure 8.1). Measurements are taken for each shape and the interior surface area determined from plane geometry formula. The depth of the stain is taken as 1 centimeter. All figures are added to arrive at a total. The advantages are that no special equipment is necessary. A tape measure and sketch pad can be used. The disadvantages are that geometry formulas must be memorized, or a reference available in the field, and that the surface area may not relate to the actual volume.

Figure 8.1

A round volume stain is found on a thin foam-backed carpet. No seepage occurred so the material lends itself to plane geometry calculations.

The latter is a serious limitation. The use of a depth of 1 in calculations, i.e. the volume is accepted as equal to the surface area, may not be valid. If the surface area of a volume stain is found to be 500 cm^2, the volume is taken as 500 cm^3. If the depth of the stain is actually 2 cm, the error is 100% under, or half the actual volume. If the depth of the volume stain is 0.5 cm, the estimate is 100% over, or double the actual amount. Underestimation is usually not as serious as overestimation. Reports should state the amount as a *minimum volume of X cc*. Observations of the actual depth is more reliable than assuming it to be '1'. If the blood is still liquid, the depth can be measured with a wooden stick. As long as the depth is 1 or greater, minimum statements based on surface area should be correct.

Absorbent material such as carpets and bedding materials provide difficulties in measuring blood stain depths. Experience with bloodstain workshops and experimentation suggest it is more reliable to accept a depth of 1 than attempt to calculate a depth. Volume stains may also vary greatly from uniform geometric shape, making alignment of dimensions difficult.

An improvement to the geometric method is more often applied now. Material similar to the crime scene evidence is used to form a volume stain of about the same size and dimensions. Both known and unknown are measured and compared. Here the type of blood should be human whole blood, which is less common than packed cells at blood banks. Packed cells would provide less soak in than crime scene bleeding and perhaps affect the final estimate. The length of time for bleeding can also interfere with interpretation.

USE OF GRID

An easier and perhaps more reliable alternative to constructing geometric shapes is the use of a prepared grid. A plastic sheet is scored in measured blocks, using inches or centimeters. The grid is positioned over the whole stain without touching the blood, and the number of blocks covering the stain is counted (see Figure 8.2). This works well with irregular stains, and plane geometry formulas are not necessary. The disadvantage again is that the depth is taken as 1. A grid must be prepared and carried to the scene. Lightweight but clear and

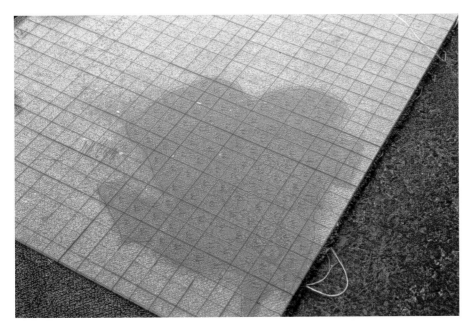

Figure 8.2

A grid divided in inch blocks is used to measure an irregular volume stain. Square inches must be converted to square centimeters before interpretation is attempted.

strong plastic is preferred but can be expensive. Markings made in inches require a conversion factor to arrive at a metric measurement for blood volume. Metric grids are smaller and require more counting. A dry marker or water soluble felt tip pen may be used to mark the squares counted.

PHOTOGRAPHIC WEIGHT

A different technique is applied to photographs with scales at right angles to the stain.[3] A unit of the photograph is cut (such as a square centimeter from the photographed scale) and weighed. The entire bloodstain in the photograph is cut out and also weighed. The unit area weight is divided into the total stain weight. The quotient is the volume of blood represented by the stain. The advantage is that a volume can be arrived at when the evidence is lost or no longer useful for examination. The disadvantages are the same as for the previous methods involving the assumption of a depth of 1. An additional disadvantage is that the investigator can not examine the volume stain to verify depth and characteristics. Oblique photographs require calculations which can further affect estimates (see Figure 8.3).

Figure 8.3

A unit of a tape measure and the whole of a volume bloodstain are cut from a photograph and weighed. Total volume is estimated as the number of unit area weights contained in the volume stain.

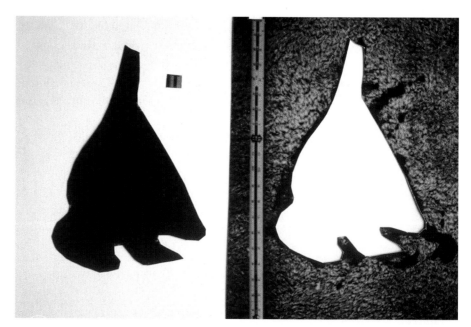

DRY WEIGHT

Dry weight determinations are more accurate yet more complicated than surface area estimates. With blood soaking through several layers of material, this is the method of choice. The material must be thoroughly dry before being processed. The whole stained area is cut out with an excess of 2 inches of border. Care must be taken not to dislodge dried blood flakes. The stained area is arranged over plastic wrap or waxed paper which in turn is placed over another area of the same material devoid of blood. The two layers separated by plastic or waxed paper are cut out together so that they are the same size. The unstained portion must be exactly the same size and shape as the stained

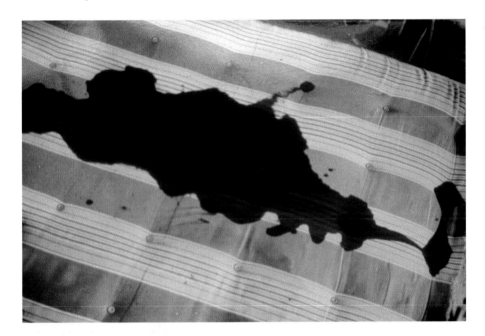

Figure 8.4
A volume bloodstain is shown on a mattress.

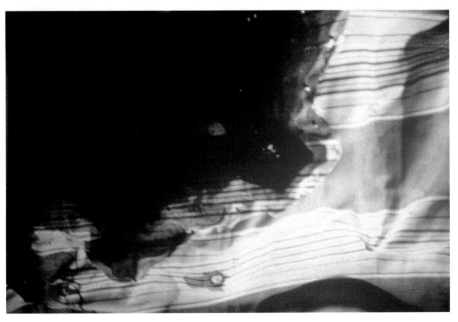

Figure 8.5
The blood area of the mattress cover is cut leaving a wide border, then positioned over the reverse side of the mattress where no bloodstains are found.

Figure 8.6

The bloodstained area is cut out with the unstained area producing an unstained blank weight to subtract from the volume stain material. The remainder is the dry weight of blood alone.

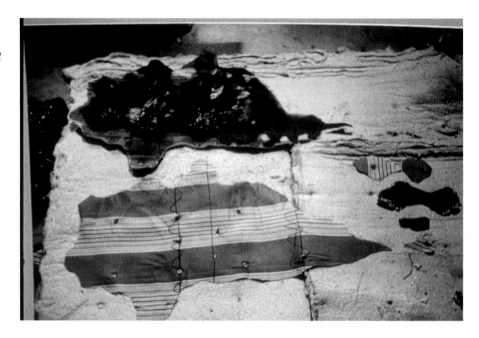

portion. This provides a blank weight of the material. The blood free blank is subtracted from the volume stained material to yield a dry weight of blood alone (see Figure 8.4–8.6).

The limitation of this technique is in the construction of a standard curve to use for estimate of volume. All dried blood samples do not weigh the same. Blood concentrated with red cells will be heavier than that which is poor in red cells. Healthy crime lab volunteers may not provide an accurate comparison for individuals such as drug and alcohol addicted victims, illegally aborted fetuses, women having traumatic miscarriage or abortion, people having a heart attack during assault, or people who have recently spent time at high altitudes. Out-of-date transfusion pouches and anticoagulated laboratory specimens contain hygroscopic salts which take up moisture from the air. Dry weight control determinations in humid climates can fluctuate too much to permit a set end point. Actual crime scene blood volume which has clotted and dried is not hygroscopic.

A standard curve for dry weight of blood is more reliable with large (50 cm^3 or more) amounts of blood. Single drop estimates are not reliable as standards for crime scene evidence. Since obtaining large quantities of volunteer blood is difficult, dangerous (without infectious disease testing), and a waste of life saving substance, an alternative should be considered. Most large volume anticoagulants depend on temporarily removing calcium from availability in the clotting cascade. It is possible to force clotting with excess calcium. This can be obtained by adding shaved blackboard chalk to anticoagulated blood. The calcium dust itself is negligible in weight when used with large volumes of blood.[b] A standard curve might be made using EDTA anticoagulated samples for a range of hematocrits. Universal blood borne pathogen precautions would be necessary in handling control samples.

Dried blood from hard, nonabsorbent surfaces may be scraped off, collected and weighed for a calculation of volume. The essential part of the technique is the standard curve or unit weight. For large stains, 500 cm^3 or more, dry weight can provide an estimate of minimum volume. For small stains and spatters, dry weight determinations are not recommended.

The author has had several situations where investigators wished to estimate volume in stains that have been washed. There is no way that a reliable initial volume estimate can be suggested for an area subjected to cleaning techniques. In some cases calculating the surface area will show the investigator that the maximum amount that could be present would not be of significance.

INTERPRETATIONS

If a reasonable estimate of the minimum bloodshed is determined, a number of interpretations may be possible. Volume blood is another time sequence indicator. Blood must be shed and fill a pool over a time interval. The most common finding is if a body is lying in a volume stain. This usually confirms that the victim bled in the position in which the body is found. Since blood may seep from injuries after death, the amount of blood in the volume stain may be significant to interpretation. If there is little or no blood around and under the body, yet flows (PABS/DRY) and autopsy results suggest volume blood loss, it is concluded that the assault occurred elsewhere and the body was moved to the location found at a time period after blood stopped flowing.

Volume bloodstains have another use. Since blood is vital to life, great loss has effects on the functions of the victim. Medical books are available with scales of normal whole body blood volumes.[4] Corrections are often listed for obesity and abnormal body forms. In general a normal healthy adult will have 70 cm^3 of blood per kilogram of weight (30 cm^3 per pound). A 25% loss of the total blood volume may be survived if loss is slow and replacement occurs before organ (heart, kidney, liver) malfunction. A rapid loss of 33% without immediate transfusion and fluid restoration should be fatal.[7] No conclusions should be based on this information without consulting a physician or medical specialist.

Since speed of blood loss influences the victim's survival, it may be important to estimate how the loss occurred. If the stain is circular or oval around the blood source (victim's injury), a moderate, steady flow is indicated. In this situation the flow pushes out evenly and forms a circular pattern. If the surface where the body is positioned slants, the pattern will be more oval. If the volume stain is very irregular with satellite spattering, rapid bleeding is suggested,

[b]The author had 95% correlation with 2000 cm^3 on a mattress and 650 cm^3 on a carpet with this technique. Workshop exercises were inconsistent and unreliable with student estimates.

perhaps arterial damage in origin. Slow bleeding, seepage, may have taken hours between the victim being in position and the body being found. Arterial gush patterns can form a volume stain in seconds or minutes. Transfer patterns involving a volume stain as the blood source depend on when and how volume accumulated.

Flow lines from wounds on the victim's body (discussed in the section on PABS/DRY) may also be noted in relation to volume stains found near a body. A pathologist should be consulted regarding whether or not blood could have drained into the body cavity rather than out into volume stains. Flow lines, however, which do not connect to pools near the body suggest it was moved after the flows stopped.

Figure 8.7 shows a volume stain which resulted predominantly from bleeding from a jugular vein. Patterns within the stain showed that a number of other events occurred while the blood was clotting.

The essential factor regarding use of volume patterns is that they are not ignored, and that they are recognized as sources of information. Each blood-stain at a crime scene provides corroboration for other stains and other physical evidence. The input of new information is a requirement of science disciplines.

Figure 8.7

Volume stain is found with the blood source of an injury to a jugular vein. Note marks within the stain show movement and transfers from a finger drawn through the clot firming pool.

REFERENCES

1. James, Stuart H. and Eckert, William G. (1989) *Interpretation of Bloodstain Evidence at Crime Scenes.* Elsevier, Amsterdam, p. 69.

2. Bevel, Tom and Gardner, Ross M. (1997) *Bloodstain Pattern Analysis.* CRC, Boca Raton, FL, pp. 189–190.

3. Lee, Henry C., Gaensslen, R.E and Pagliaro, Elaine M. (1986) 'Blood volume estimation', *International Association of Bloodstain Pattern Analysts News* **3**(2), 47–55.

4. Tietz, Norbert W. (1983) *Clinical Guide to Laboratory Tests.* W.B. Saunders, Philadelphia, pp. 88–89.

5. Sohmer, Paul R. (1979) 'The pathophysiology of hemorrhagic shock', in *Hemotherapy in Trauma and Surgery.* American Association of Blood Banks, Washington, DC, p. 1.

A struggle composite is shown.

CHAPTER 9

COMPOSITE BLOODSTAIN PATTERNS

[a]Crime scene photograph from G. Michele Yezzo, Ohio BCI&I.

Violent events involving bloodshed usually involve several different, often overlapping, patterns. Investigators may err by assuming that arrangements of spatters always represent single actions.[1] To discourage lumping all stains under one term (such as *Medium Velocity Impact Spatters*), thus speeding identification and interpretation, an additional bloodstain pattern category is suggested: *composites*. The heading includes frequently encountered overlapping combinations from both spatter and nonspatter groups. Identification may be made of complex events.

GUNSHOT DISPERSED IMPACT SPATTER

Although gunshot distributes Impact Spatter patterns, each shot is not limited to only one event. Students of bloodstain pattern workshops show a remarkable ability to identify gunshot dispersed Impact Spatter, even in the absence of specific training exercises in the program. Detectives with homicide experience tend to score better than criminalists and identification technicians for gunshot pattern identification. This indicates that there are visual characteristics of gunshot Impact Spatter patterns that set them apart from other impact events, and which may become part of an investigator's knowledge.

The components of a fired bullet have been recorded[2] as similar to those in Figure 9.1. Gases associated with weapon discharge, as well as the bullet, may cause blood drop separation and distribution. Impact spatter patterns resulting from gunshot are combinations of contact between an exposed blood source, the bullet (missile), and gas components. The components are identified as:

- Preblast (gas)
- Capsular blast (gas)
- Bullet entrance (missile)
- Muzzle blast (gas)
- Bullet exit (missile/missile fragments)

Figure 9.1

An artist's sketch shows possible components for multiple impacts from a fired bullet.

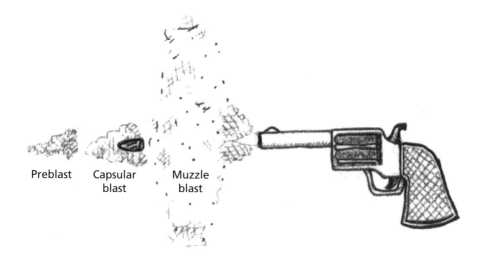

Figure 9.1

An artist's sketch shows possible components for multiple impacts from a fired bullet.

The bullet may expose the blood source or strike prior exposed blood. If the source is not available until impact by the bullet, preblast and capsular blast are not recorded. If the gunshot occurs within a stationary system, immobile victim, target, and firearm, the composite parts to entrance wound will be recorded as one overlapping pattern. If movement occurs, especially rapid movement, the separate parts of the composite may strike different areas and indicate different origins for the entrance wound alone. If this is the case, measurable stains are more likely to represent the origin of bullet penetration, while atomized and explosive spatter stains (streaks and exclamation mark shapes) will indicate the origin immediately after the bullet impact. Clearly it will be essential to all gunshot spatter patterns to note the conditions of the blood source (injury) before drawing conclusions.

An experiment was conducted using a fixed mounted 0.38 caliber handgun and fixed exposed blood source (cardboard strip with blood soaked thin sponge attached). The recording target was spinning at a rate of approximately 12 miles per hour. Separated spatter patterns were recorded consistent with the composite illustration (see Figures 9.2–9.4).

Investigators lacking a scientific background often equate mist sized spatters with gunshot spatter patterns. Mist has been equated to results from a 'high velocity bullet'. It is true that gunshot may create a greater degree of drop separation, smaller size and larger overall density of spatters, than such events as bludgeoning. Mist, however, does not depend on the speed of the bullet. Gunshot spatter patterns may be duplicated with an artist spray brush assembly where no bullet is involved. The similarity in pattern results from similar dynamics, a gas (muzzle blast) meets a blood source (exposed by the bullet) and atomizes it. Mist patterns are described as looking atomized or 'spray painted' because they are essentially atomized by expanding gases.

Figure 9.2

The system arranged to detect separate impacts from a single gunshot.

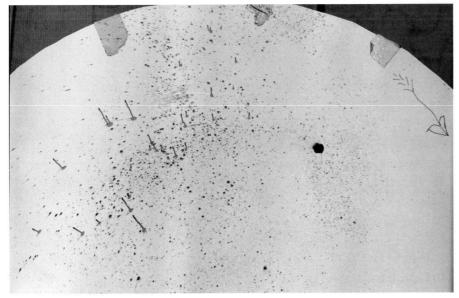

Figure 9.3

A section of the target shows areas of spatter dispersed by different parts of the gunshot.

IDENTIFICATION OF GUNSHOT IMPACT SPATTER

The key to identifying a gunshot spatter pattern is that it represents characteristics of a recognizable composite,[3] which includes two or more of the following characteristics:

- Predominant mist and/or fine spatters in the pattern.
- The area of convergence approaches a point per missile at the entrance to the blood source.

Figure 9.4

A close up is shown of the spinning target. The preblast and capsular blast are indicated.

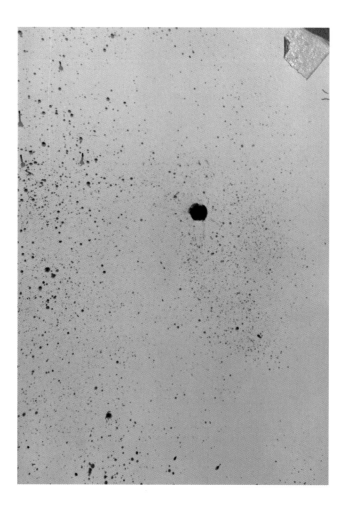

- ■ Secondary spatters appear as streaks rather than dots.
- ■ Gunshot (explosive) residue is found within the pattern.
- ■ Elimination based on physical evidence of alternative impact events.

Another caution against equating gunshot impact spatter with mist is that mist sized spatters may result from actions other than gunshot. A small artery of a victim with greatly elevated blood pressure may show mist sized spatter upon breach with no bullet involved. Wheeze and sneeze may also project mist sized spatter. Identifying gunshot in terms of spatter size ranges alone may lead to incorrect conclusions. On the other hand, failing to identify gunshot from the lack of mist spatters ignores other identifying characteristics. Mist size drops may fail to be recorded at the scene. Labeling a gunshot composite pattern as mist spatter simply because the terms are considered synonymous is subjective application of the evidence.

Angular considerations are essential in evaluating the presence or absence of mist spatter in a gunshot impact scenario. A single bullet may project blood drops in a cone shaped array, much like the spray hose attachment seen in Figure 9.5. The cone will intersect targets in a triangular, or 'V' shaped pattern. There will be an absence of spatters between the area of convergence and where spatters are recorded because of the shape of the projected array. This is a caution in interpreting blockage transfer patterns. A consequence of this arrangement is that occasionally the edge of the cone array is recorded in a linear overall pattern. When this happens the pattern may resemble cast off. This is encountered with gunshots in vehicles because of the low head space. The distance from the origin results in fewer size ranges, and medium sized drops carry well, therefore the pattern may also show a uniform size of spatters characteristic of Swing Cast Off. Differentiation is possible by constructing an Area of Convergence. With swing Cast Offs there will be a shift of the lines crossing over the range of the pattern. For the gunshot Impact Spatter pattern no Direction of Travel may be seen since drop impacts are at right angles.

The properties of the gun must be considered. Gases projected out of the sides of a weapon[4] can have a misting effect on exposed blood sources. In addition, gunshots often involve secondary events such as Cast Offs from a falling victim, and/or bloodstained hair strands. Rapid dripping from injuries may produce another composite: *Blood into Blood*.

Figure 9.5
A garden hose projection resembles cone shaped blood distribution by a bullet entrance.

BLOOD INTO BLOOD

The effects of Blood into Blood are commonly recognized.[5-7] A volume stain is found surrounded by considerable numbers of satellite spatters (see Figure

9.6). A variance is observed based on the rate of drip. Figure 9.7 shows a comparison between slow and rapid drip with all other parameters held constant. The beakers measured 6 inches in height; all conditions were the same for both systems except for frequency and time of drip. Although the time each system was allowed to drip was different, the height and distribution of spatters did not change. The only difference with time was the number of spatters recorded. For a slow rate the majority of spatters recorded were within 2.5 inches of the bottom, while fast rate satellite drops cleared the 6 inch container and left small and fine spatters on the counter surface outside it. Clearly, if crime scene evidence indicates Blood into Blood, the nature of injuries and rate of bleed becomes important. The size and distance traveled by spatters is in the same range as that accepted as Impact Spatter, blunt force and gunshot. Contact with Blood into Blood can implicate individuals in and around a bleeding victim. The distance drops fall does not influence the scatter as much as the rate. Soft absorbent surfaces may dampen scatter but rate of bleed is still a key to interpretation. If drip is fast enough to form a pool on a carpet surface, distribution will be independent of the soft surface. Satellite spatters, however, may be difficult to see.

Blood into blood includes a composite of:

- *Impact* (Blood drop impacts blood source)
- *Cast Off* (Dripping is a cast off dynamics)
- (*Arterial Damage*, possible blood source, but not required).

IDENTIFICATION OF BLOOD INTO BLOOD

Recognition of blood into blood patterns involves noting the randomness of Directions of Travel for satellite spatter distributed from a volume bloodstain. Secondary drops originate from anywhere around the volume stain, yet the circumference continues to expand as blood is added. This contributes to satellite spatters appearing to originate from random areas. If the volume stain initiates coagulation while Drip Cast Offs continue to fall, spatters may be connected to the pool by thin fibrin strands. This may have given rise to the assumption that Blood into Blood satellites have Directions of Travel toward the blood source rather than away from it as other Impact patterns show.

Investigators need to be aware that such spatters can be found on the underside of adjacent objects. Secondary spatters after a drop strikes the pool are also distributed horizontally depending upon the size of the pool. With prolonged, rapid dripping, Blood into Blood patterns have been recorded to cover an 8 ft^2 floor.[b] A pulsing artery may spray into a volume bloodstain projecting satellite streaks resembling Splash.

[b]Photogrammetry exhibit seen in New South Wales Police Department CID October 1990.

Figure 9.6

A blood into blood composite pattern is shown.

Figure 9.7

Blood drops from an outdated packed cell transfusion pouch (75% hematocrit) positioned 36 inches over clear plastic beakers. Blood drops were allowed to fall by gravity alone from an IV line. Variance was only in the rate and time interval of drip. Beaker B (right) rate was 1 drop/5 seconds for 10 minutes. Beaker A (left) rate was approximately 7 drops per second for 30 seconds.

ARTERIAL DAMAGE

Blood into blood patterns may be included as parts of other composites, such as an Arterial Damage composite. The dynamics which distribute spatters by arterial blood vessel pressure was discussed in Chapter 5, but a composite is also recognized. When one pattern is found, others should be recognized or noted for their presence or absence.

IDENTIFICATION OF ARTERIAL DAMAGE COMPOSITE PATTERNS

Two or more of the following components indicate an arterial damage composite. Note that arterial fountain and arterial breach patterns are omitted because of the possible confusion with other pattern types.

Bright red colored blood volume or wet stains
Volume
Blood into Blood
Arterial Spurt/Gush
Arterial Rain

Figure 9.8

The car door panel shows an arterial damage composite: arterial spurts, volume, and blood into blood. A victim suffered a self-inflicted gunshot wound to the deltoid artery.

With the composite Arterial Damage pattern, investigators must verify artery location with a physician. In Figure 9.8 no mention was made of arterial damage until after the scene was viewed. Medical records reviewed later showed the injury was to the deltoid artery.

STRUGGLE

Violent crimes are often scenes of considerable activity. Defensive gestures and struggles between assailants and victims occur. See the Frontispiece for an example. A composite of actions may be recognized:

- Moving Transfers (usually as wipes and/or swipes in an arc or curved shape)
- Scattered Drip/Swing Cast Offs
- Direct Transfers (shoe and/or foot prints are common, but arm and hair may be seen)

Since the composite involves Drip Cast Offs it is usually found on the floor or ground. Other parts of the composite may be found either on the floor/ground or vertical surfaces. It consists of low velocity Swing Cast Off (individual spatters show gravitational pull downward) and Drip Cast Off, interspersed with Moving Transfers and Smudges. Shoe and foot sole, and edges may be found in proximity with the other pattern groups (see Figure 9.9).

Figure 9.9

A struggle composite is identified from curved moving transfers, especially since they pass over scattered drip cast offs. Duplicate shoe transfers show action suggestive of shoving off balance.

CONTAMINATION/IT (INVESTIGATIVE TRANSFER)

Too often investigators ignore bloodstain patterns which they suspect or know have resulted after the crime was discovered. Experience has shown that sooner or later these stains will have to be acknowledged. Less embarrassment will result if they are identified and interpreted as early as possible in the investigation. Patterns involved in IT/Contamination include:

- Volume
- PABS/dry and/or PABS/clot
- Transfers, usually simple direct
- Drip Cast Offs
- Splash Impact Spatters

Two events are recorded in Figure 9.10. One occurred with fresh blood, while a second involved only serum. This could suggest Investigative Transfer, contamination, or an assailant remaining at the crime scene for a period of time.

Figure 9.10

Two impacts occurred with a time span between. Note subtle serum streaks.

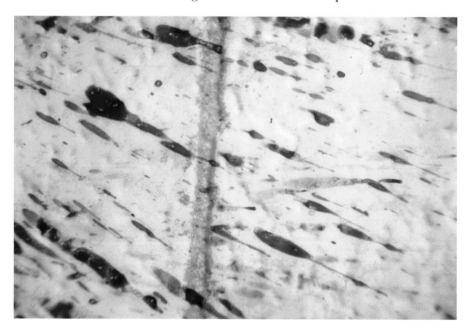

Even though contamination and Investigative Transfers are potentially destructive, the patterns may be useful in developing a time line. Cases are encountered where contamination is alleged by the assailant to explain transfers and bloodstains upon the person. Other uses include the recognition that moving transfers show that blood was still moist when paramedics or others arrived at the scene. Drying times can be determined by noting when IT was and was not possible. All bloodstain pattern evidence is useful in *reconstructing* events.

SECONDARY, SATELLITE, AND RICOCHET DROPS

Often drop separation and deposit on a target lead to minor subsequent events. While these may have no significance to the crime scene, they may create confusion in identification and interpretation of major patterns. The terms satellite and secondary are often interchanged. Secondary drop used here has referred to single drops distributed in association with a *parent drop*, while satellites referred to many fine drops distributed around a stain.

SECONDARY DROPS

A second fine, small, or medium sized drop is formed when a larger, parent, drop hits a target surface. The secondary drop is distributed beyond this, in the Direction of Travel. With drops hitting a target at high velocity, secondary drops may be separated by some distance from the parent, and/or be recorded as streaks and/or exclamation marks instead of dots. Another type of secondary drop was discussed in Chapter 2. A second drop may separate at the same time as the parent drop.[8] The process is not as dependent upon gravity,[9] as it is on viscosity and elasticity of the fluid. With more viscoelastic fluids, the thread attaching the parent drop to the fluid source elongates. For Drip Cast Offs, the smaller mass of the secondary drop slows faster than the parent and results in it falling slightly behind the larger stain.

SATELLITE SPATTER

Two situations always involve satellite spatter, Arterial Gush and Blood into Blood. The dynamics of formation are described in the relevant chapters. Excess satellite spatters may obscure details of other dynamic acts. It is essential that this be recognized for what it is and not mistaken for the products of such events as Impact Spatter. Drip Cast Offs may occasionally involve multiple drops which show Blood into Blood type of satellite spatters. Individual Drip Cast Offs may also have satellite spatter as part of the edge characteristics in situations such as when the drops are large and the target surface is rough.

RICOCHET

Whether the term *ricochet* is applicable or not has been debated. What is usually seen is that a drop breaks up upon hitting a target with the products of break up directed away from the target surface. When there is an overlap of many ricochet secondary spatters, confusion may result in calling the appearance mist spatter. Closely examining the surface usually resolves the question.

APPLICATION AND RECORDING OF COMPOSITE PATTERNS

Although the composite patterns are useful to speed interpretation, the parts of any composite should also be recorded. A struggle may be recognized, but the interpretation of details depends upon analysis of all component patterns. For example, defensive actions from a victim may result in the composite of struggle, but so would efforts to move an unconscious victim. The patterns within the composition of struggle could aid in differentiating these acts. Defensive gestures may include cessation cast offs not common to struggle in moving an inert body. All bloodstain patterns contribute to a complete reconstruction of events.

REFERENCES

1. Chisum, J. (1998) *Pitfalls in Bloodstain Pattern Interpretation.* California Association of Criminalists Spring Meeting, Monterey.

2. Vincent DiMaio (1999) *Gunshot Wounds* (2nd edn). CRC, Boca Raton, FL, p. 49.

3. Wonder, Anita Y. (1994) *An Objective Approach to the Identification of Gunshot Impact Spatter Patterns.* American Academy of Forensic Sciences Annual Meeting, San Antonio, Texas.

4. Vincent DiMaio (1999) *Gunshot Wounds* (2nd edn). CRC, Boca Raton, FL, p. 51.

5. MacDonell, Herbert L. (1982) *Bloodstain Pattern Interpretation.* Laboratory of Forensic Science, Corning, NY, p. 11.

6. Bevel, Tom and Gardner, Ross M. (1997) *Bloodstain Pattern Analysis with an Introduction to Crime Scene Reconstruction.* CRC, Boca Raton, FL, pp. 190–195.

7. James, Stuart H. (1989) *Interpretation of Bloodstain Evidence at Crime Scenes.* Elsevier, Amsterdam, p. 19.

8. Sears, Francis Weston, and Zemansky, Mark W. (1955) *University Physics.* Complete Edition. Addison-Wesley, Reading, Massachusetts, p. 229.

9. Padday, J.P. (1996) *Dynamics of Multiphase Flows Across Interfaces* (Ed. Annie Steinchen). Springer-Verlag, Berlin, p. 41.

A reconstruction of the crime scene shown in the Frontispiece to Chapter 2 was made.

CHAPTER 10

RECONSTRUCTION

Dr Paul Kirk introduced the term 'Reconstruction' into his presentation before the California Trial Lawyer's Association in 1968. He pointed out that courts attempt to limit expert testimony to statements of facts without interpretation. Dr Kirk explained the need for reconstruction and interpretation from qualified experts:

> There is the legal fiction that the judge and jury must interpret the facts established by all witnesses, including experts. This, in many cases, is literally asking the blind to lead the blind.[1]

Courts continue to grapple with the reality of bloodstain pattern evidence. Four of the attitudes which may be encountered include:

- Require measurements and data records but deny interpretation.
- Require reconstruction experimentation, often with emphasis on *pattern match*.
- Allow everything into record to be debated as to the weight of the evidence.
- Ignore the evidence and focus on the qualifications of the expert.

Because courts may approach the evidence in these ways, attorneys appearing in those courts favor experts who fit their work to the attitude. Unfortunately many individuals believe that these are the only ways to handle bloodstain pattern evidence. Actually, none of the four need to be based on scientific methodology. Measurements may be presented which are incorrect or applied out of context, such as Cast Off bloodspatters measured for Impact Origin location. Pattern match illustrations may be manipulated with dynamics not involved in a particular case. Too often judges and juries feel confident if the first two approaches are applied. The third, however, is more likely to be a just format if the adversary approach is followed with competent experts appearing for both sides. Decisions handed down by the *triers of fact* (judges and juries) suggest they are not always impressed with the quantity and quality of previous court appearances.

Without formal criteria for identifying bloodstain patterns, the validity of testimony defaults to individual Curriculum vitae. An expert may have worked on hundreds of cases without having received even basic training. The volume of casework does not determine quality of methodology, nor does lack of experience determine inability to apply science. An analogy is the student of astronomy. An outdoors person such as a hunter or fisherman may have years more experience but not be able to state anything regarding a photograph of a star-filled night sky. The astronomy student with little outdoors experience but good education can provide expert advice. The key, of course, is training followed by experience. Dr Kirk expressed this concern for forensic experts.

RECONSTRUCTION APPROACHES

The reconstruction process has developed to the extent that it is being recognized as an independent step in crime scene investigation. Reconstruction of a crime or crime scene usually involves at least three approaches:

- Solving the crime or crimes by graphically reconstructing a series of events
- Applying techniques to reconstruct individual events
- Conducting experiments to reproduce characteristics of bloodstain patterns

SOLVING THE CRIME

IDENTIFICATION

There are two approaches to bloodstain pattern identification, with various combinations of both encountered. The approaches may be labeled *subjective analysis* and *objective analysis.*

In subjective analysis, investigators develop a scenario based on witness statements, previous experience, and other evidence such as fingerprints and autopsy reports. Bloodstain patterns are labeled according to the scenario. Identification may be correct if witnesses are truthful, the investigators are good detectives, and other evidence is relevant to the crime under investigation. This type of approach is pervasive. Experts who apply analysis subjectively often impress their employers because they provide the desired answers, and thus are repeatedly hired.

The problem with subjective identification is that the bloodstains are not used in the identification process. The validity of patterns depends on characteristics other than the bloodstains themselves. If witnesses lie, investigators are wrong, and/or other evidence misinterpreted, information from bloodstain patterns is also lost. Since bloodstain patterns used properly can contribute to investigative leads, the subjective approach is a waste of useful evidence. Additionally, if other information, used to develop the scenario, is impeached in court the bloodstains based upon them are also impeached. A whole case can be lost, or subsequent embarrassment result, purely from subjective approaches. This is not the only approach to the evidence available.

An objective analysis of bloodstain patterns identifies evidence on the basis of characteristics of the bloodstains themselves. Identification is not linked to other evidence until after identification of the bloodstain patterns, that is, after identification of patterns but before case interpretation. Bloodstain patterns can be applied to corroborate or refute witness statements, detective hunches, and/or the meaning of other physical evidence before a scenario is developed. This is the purpose of the objective criteria approach in the identification of bloodstain patterns.

SEQUENCING

Crimes where blood is shed will involve a *time line*. Stages usually include a minimum of three events:

- Blood source exposed
- Blood distributed
- Crime scene discovered

These may occur in rapid succession or span hours, days, or longer with additional events occurring between or after stages. The major bloodstain pattern group headings can be sequenced relative to the stages.

BLOOD SOURCE EXPOSED

Impact and Arterial Breach are events which expose a blood source. These, if found, orient the crime *toward the beginning of events*. If a series of assaults are suspected, finding an Impact pattern may only identify where one event occurred. Other events may have involved too little exposed blood to distribute recordable drops. The amount of blood in the patterns can assist sequencing of serial events: the less blood, the closer to the beginning of an assault. Again, a caution is indicated. An impact to a blood source may occur, followed by an impact to an area not yet bloodied. The second would involve fewer, or no, spatters. Examining areas of the scene and the victim's clothing for Transfer patterns may help identify sequence of blows and confirm the probable number of impacts.

DISTRIBUTING EVENTS

The spatter groups and some of the PABS and composites involve distribution of drops. Transfers produce pattern match evidence. These must occur after a blood source has been exposed but while blood remains liquid and available for distribution. Directions of Travel are used to reconstruct the direction in which victims and/or assailants move after blood is shed.

CRIME SCENE DISCOVERY

The scene may be discovered immediately or lie undiscovered for a time before being discovered. Volume blood may play a part in determining how long a victim has remained in a single location, and indicate whether or not the body was moved. PABS will develop from drying of stains, clotting of blood, through distribution of blood substance by flies and other insects, or other inter-mingling with environmental factors including dirt, leaves, water, etc., inside and outside. Such evidence provides a boundary of applicable patterns. Investigative transfer may confuse the issue and should be identified and eliminated rather than ignored. Sequencing Investigative Transfer and contamination may even assist in a time line for the crime events, such as shoe prints over completely dried versus partially dried spatters.

SEQUENCING PAIRS

Each of the major pattern groups may be linked to at least one other group. For example, Impact Spatters result near the start of the opening of a blood source, but if the event is beating, a close second pattern of Cast Off will result. Finding impact spatters indicates that it is advisable to check for Cast Offs too. Finding any one Arterial Damage pattern suggests that there may be other variations including the Blood into Blood composite, Impact Spatter, and Blood into Blood outline Blockage patterns. Some of this information is used in developing composite pattern types. Pairs and groups, in order of expected occurrence during events, are suggested in the list below:

Stage 1
Impact Spatter/Swing Cast Offs
Arterial Gush/Arterial Spurt/Arterial Rain/Blood into Blood/Volume blood

Stage 2
Drip Cast Offs/Moving Transfers/Blood into Blood/Blockage transfers
Simple Direct Transfers (pattern match trace evidence)
Arterial Damage (continued action)

Stage 3
Volume blood
PABS/dry, clot, mix/insect distribution

After Stage 3
IT and contamination

LIMITATIONS IN CONCLUSIONS

As indicated above, reconstruction and scenario development must continually be evaluated for subjectivity. The process is one of identifying patterns, sequencing them with respect to other patterns, comparing with other physical evidence, developing possible scenarios, testing and eliminating impossible scenarios, and limiting conclusions to those facts confirmed or which can not be excluded. It must be stated that although a reconstructed scenario may appear to fit all the bloodstain patterns identified, there is always a possibility that another scenario could also fit the evidence. The more patterns identified and corroborated, the more one can limit the possibilities of alternative reconstructions.

RECONSTRUCTION TECHNIQUES

Each major pattern category provides information for a crime reconstruction. The information provided is free at a crime scene. Not to evaluate and apply it is a waste of valuable evidence. Some methodologies have been applied to bloodstain patterns to increase and illustrate the available information relative to the *corpus delicti* (body of the crime).

IMPACT SPATTERS

An impact is a single event which locates a dynamic act in one interval of time and space. Although a time span is involved, it is so short as to be instantaneous for all practical purposes. The most common use is to locate a victim and an assailant in a specific area of space at the precise time of a forceful strike to a blood source. To arrive at the origin of a group of Impact Spatters, measurements are taken. The results may provide one or more origins where impacts occurred. The size and shape of Areas of Convergence relate to the size and shape of blows to the blood source. Early blows will have a relatively smaller Area of Convergence because the area of exposed blood is smaller. As injuries are inflicted, more blood is available over a wider area, i.e. larger relative areas of convergence will be found. This may be used to sequence multiple blows.

The size of the event between weapon and injury may also suggest the size and shape of a weapon used in bludgeoning. The Areas of Convergence can be used to corroborate reconstruction of the origin. Unfortunately most computer assisted origin reconstruction programs eliminate Areas of Convergence.

The technique of string reconstruction is applied to impact spatter patterns. It is a time consuming and often tedious procedure but may provide highly probative information. Although some individuals claim they can do a string reconstruction alone, best results are obtained using a team of three approach. The procedure should be included with basic bloodstain pattern workshops. Improvements exist in which laser beams are used instead of strings.

Computer applications are advocated by technical investigators. These programs speed applications and help eliminate some human error in calculations. Unfortunately, computers do not yet identify patterns nor choose and measure appropriate stains. Advocates of computer applications have stated that it does not matter whether stains are Impact or Cast Offs. Workshops where mock crime scenes are created and analyzed over years of practice refute this assumption.

CAST OFF RE-ENACTMENTS

Too often extreme care is taken to form a mock crime scene with the same materials present at a case scene, but less care is taken in the actual dynamics. In gaining an understanding of the crime it is more important that the weapon and the 'assailant' used in Cast Off distribution be as close to the actual weapon/wielder of the weapon as possible. The way a prospective weapon is normally used must be considered. Situations have been reviewed where hammers were alleged to have been used like ball bats, and knives used like tire irons. The benefit from re-enactment is lost if the dynamics bear little or no relationship to the crime alleged.

ARTERIAL DAMAGE DEMONSTRATIONS

Arterial patterns may be demonstrated with a syringe and needle or a pump device. Some instructors use a peristaltic pump design. These create patterns resembling Arterial Spurts but the principle is not the same. Pumps move fluid along with periodic breaks in pressure, while arteries are under constant pressure with periodic surges. Attempts to manufacture a more accurate model of the heart is difficult because of commercial trade secrecy. If simple illustration and/or basic training is the objective, the differences between recirculating and peristaltic pumps are not enough for concern.

TRANSFERS

Transfer patterns are *pattern match* evidence. Specific patterns are widely recognized and used in crime reconstruction, such as finger prints, foot and shoe impressions, fabric and stitch patterns, and tool marks. Photography with scales, camera positioned at right angles, and frame filled are essential in recording, analyzing, and illustrating specific patterns. Sequences are enhanced with partial drying and overlapping bloodstains which may be difficult to see with the unaided eye. Alternative light sources and chemical enhancements may be applied, especially to transfers, in reconstructing events which may include attempts to hide or destroy bloodstain evidence.

PABS

Physiologically Altered Blood Stains provide an impressive index of time sequence. Sufficient time must pass for blood to dry, clot or mix with other substances, yet this is not all. Each PABS group also involves separate stages which further define the sequence of events. PABS/clot requires sufficient volume of blood which can proceed through the coagulation process before blood dries. This is also a factor in investigative transfers and may aid in eliminating patterns which are not part of a crime sequence. Techniques such as use of wooden sticks and glass or plastic rods to test for coagulation stage can be important to a case. Reconstruction and training techniques can use chalk dust added to anticoagulated blood.

VOLUME

Although volume bloodstains are often considered the final stage of the process, PABS/clot actually follows. Volume bloodstains are necessary for clotting to be visible. Volume patterns, therefore, precede PABS/clot, and may precede other PABS patterns such as dry and mix/flyspeck. Techniques for estimating volume bloodstains are available although cautions are noted. If a pattern contains so much blood that the amount is critical to reconstruction, the dry weight method is favored. See Chapter 8 for a description of the technique.

COMPOSITE

A technique was suggested to determine the distance from a gun barrel to a blood source using a pipe cleaner to wipe the inside of the barrel.[2] Experimentation with this technique has shown that it can be manipulated. The procedure is to dampen a pipe cleaner and enclose it in a plastic straw. The straw and cleaner are inserted into a gun barrel. The straw is removed and the pipe cleaner twirled to wipe the gun barrel interior. The straw is reinserted and the assembly removed. The depth of penetration is tested using a chemical reaction to detect hemoglobin. The limitation of this technique is that the straw can transfer enough blood to provide a positive reaction, especially after it is dampened by contact with the pipe cleaner. The interpretation range is small enough that a few millimeters can indicate widely different distances between victim and weapon. Photography of the barrel interior[3] has improved to the extent that the pipe cleaner approach should no longer be a consideration.

An additional comment should be made regarding the interpretation of blood found within the gun barrel. The process of blood drops projecting into the barrel of the gun from which the bullet emerged has been referred to as *drawback* due in part to *a near vacuum in the barrel*.[4] Gun barrels are not closed systems sufficient to create a vacuum, although they may have tight fitting ammunition. The expanding gases from the muzzle blast will be immediately replaced with air from any and all crevices. The essential fact is that *drawback* and *blow back* in a gun barrel can not be differentiated, even if drawback were possible. The dynamics of blood drops distributed by gunshot does not differ in principle from beating blows.

EXPERIMENTAL DESIGN

[a]People v. Carter, 312 P2 665 (1957)

[b]Ibid.

In response to Dr Kirk's testimonies,[a] reconstruction became synonymous with experimentation to recreate bloodstain patterns which were *substantially similar* to those found at scenes of bloodshed.[b] What may be regarded as experimental observations range from oversimplified exercises during basic bloodstain pattern workshops to the design of elaborate special devices in national and international crime labs. Something may be learned regarding blood behavior from all of these, as long as limitations are also understood.

COMPONENTS

The first consideration should be to the type of blood used in the experiments. Ink, paint, glycerol and red dye, dyed commercial aquarium salt water, and animal bloods have been substituted for human blood for various reasons. Safety considerations are the primary concern but availability is a close second. From an applications viewpoint, nothing behaves exactly like human blood for training and research purposes. An example of animal blood may be seen in the British video *Blood in Slow Motion*.[5] The use of animal blood for safety concerns may provide a false sense of security. Many viruses cause benign disease in animals but serious illness in humans. If animal blood is used it must be obtained through sources familiar with animal/human disease transfers. Human blood from volunteers tested for known diseases and judged safe for transfusion is far safer than untested animal blood. Laboratory and workshop volunteers who contribute without any health testing should be viewed with caution.

Newtonian substances used instead of non-Newtonian substances will vary depending upon the factors under investigation. If these are used for simple illustrations of drop distribution under conditions of impact, cast off, and pressure projection (arterial damage), the variance of drop size and separation, spatter edge characteristics, etc. from crime dynamics is offset by safety. On the other hand, if size and distance traveled by the drop array are to be identified from the results of experimentation, substitutes are unacceptable. The behavior of whole blood compared with pack red blood cells may differ for strict numerical data records to be applied to casework.

SET UP

A common approach to reconstruction experimentation is to obtain a sample of blood (human or animal) and subject it to *similar* conditions alleged in a particular case in order to see what happens. While this might not appear scientific, it is preferable to an alternative where the end results are listed before designing the set up. The main element in any case oriented experimentation must be to observe conditions without a preconceived objective. This is especially true of Spatter Group patterns.

Because blood, time, and facilities are not easily found for all investigators, it is important that each experiment is planned and recorded for maximum benefit. The court requirement for *substantially similar* may vary considerably for those doing reconstruction experimentation. The usual emphasis is on obtaining the same materials as those found at a specific crime scene: floor, wall, window, furniture, and fabric textures. Unfortunately, the exactness of these choices may be followed by dynamics which bare little or no resemblance to the crime events. On the other hand one cannot reproduce the exact dynamics without committing the crime again, perhaps not even then. The middle ground is carefully to decide what case events are to be studied.

The frontispiece shows a reconstruction of the crime scene in the frontispiece to Chapter 2 (p. 18). Note the similarities of spatter sizes and shapes. The large oval stains seen in the Chapter 2 frontispiece are arterial damage spatters because they are uniform size ovals, perpendicular with the floor arranged symmetrically and parallel with each other in a 'V' whole pattern shape. The large ovals in the reconstruction are swing cast offs in a linear whole pattern arranged in a line. Cast offs were found at the scene with direction of travel across the door from right to left *toward the victim*. This indicated a horizontal assault which was confirmed by injuries to the victim's forehead. Reconstruction was delivered with only vertical blows. If the victim had sustained all blows vertically it is unlikely she would have survived, as fortunately she did.

Figures 10.1–10.5 show the results of a reconstruction experiment conducted to evaluate the dynamics involved when a gunshot breaches an arterial blood vessel. No specific case was being processed. A latex tubing from a recirculating pump was taped to a 3 inch square by 6 inch high wooden block. A lead unjacketed bullet from a .38 revolver was fired into the tubing perpendicular to the top of the block. The bullet passed through the tubing, flattening and stretching rather than cleaving, and split the block into two pieces. The section of block with the tubing attached tipped over. Several separate spatter patterns resulted: Arterial Gush, Arterial Spurt, Fine spatter pattern, and various Splash Impact Spatter patterns. Mist was not recorded. The fine spatter was projected to the left of the block, not back toward the position of the shooter.

The conclusions from the exercise were that there are exceptions to the belief that fine and mist spatter are only 'blown' back toward the shooter. The arterial spurt pattern reflected both the pressure from the line and the impact of the bullet; and a single event can leave several different patterns. Casework since the exercise has shown similar dynamics with recognizable variations. The analyst must view the whole scene as a composition of individual patterns.

It is a common court misconception to believe that an expert must conduct an experiment in order to identify patterns from a specific case. This equates bloodstain patterns to *pattern match* evidence. Transfer spatters are pattern match but spatter patterns are not pattern match evidence. They occur in a three-dimensional context which cannot be exactly duplicated. The analogy given is that spatter distribution during crime events is not unlike debris distribution from bomb blasts. Requiring reconstruction dynamics to distribute blood drops in the same array as a crime is no more valid than requesting a bomb explosion to determine the distribution of debris. Research has been conducted in general and for specific situations, thus is not necessary for each case. Experts have learned how to identify dynamic events from criteria seen within bloodspatter patterns. It follows that reconstruction experimentation should only be necessary for confirmation of specific questions and illustrations.

Spatter patterns may be created by a variety of techniques. Individual stain size and shape are not dependent upon specific dynamic events such as a gunshot or beating blow. Various techniques such as artist air brushes, squirt bottles, and spring trap devices can duplicate stains of various sizes at any angle desired. The amount of blood and exact nature and degree of applied force

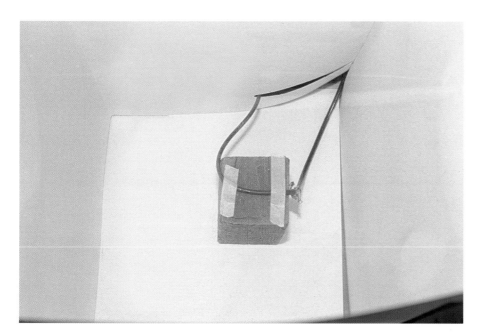

Figure 10.1
A cube arrangement is made around a 6 inch tall block. A section of latex tubing from a recirculating pump with blood extends over the top of the block.

Figure 10.2
Immediately after the shot.

from a dynamic crime event cannot be reproduced in an experiment, and certainly not if the context of a crime is not known in advance. It follows that reconstruction experimentation should not be used to identify spatter patterns. The trier of fact is not qualified to know whether or not a spatter pattern is or is not substantially similar to that of a crime alleged. To assume so can lead to serious misinterpretations.

Figure 10.3

Close up of bullet and tubing showing bullet entrance. The much larger bullet passed through the small hole by flattening and stretching the latex. Tubing was cut after the shot.

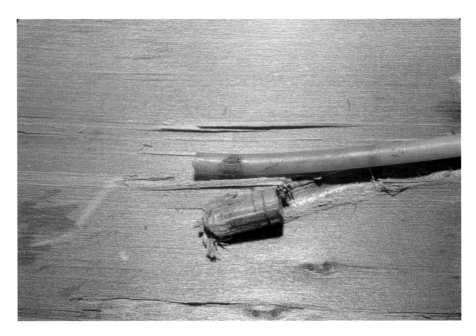

Figure 10.4

A pattern which resulted as a combined event between gunshot Impact and Arterial Spurt.

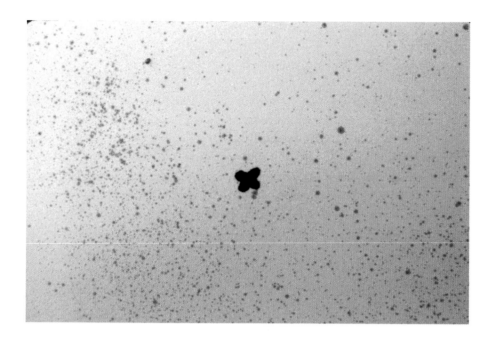

Figure 10.5
Fine spatter projected 9 inches (6 inch to block and 3 inches to tubing on the block) to the left of the right-handed shooter.

Given the conditions and cautions for designing a reconstruction experiment, what can be accomplished? The best application is an illustration of spatial relationships, techniques in handling weapons, and a time line construction. Reconstruction of blockage patterns verify that the absence of stains is due to blockage and not angle of assault. Horizontal versus vertical assaults project both swing cast offs and impact spatter patterns characteristic of the way an assault was perpetrated. Reproducing the angles and substantially similar whole patterns both inform and illustrate the probable crime scene dynamics.

INTERPRETATION

If the reconstruction experiment has been designed well, conclusions may provide information not anticipated. If results suggest that the logic from casework needs revision, that revision must be based upon facts, not speculation regarding why experimental results differ. In other words, repeat the experiment with suggested changes. Do not assume changes would provide differences between an accepted case scenario and experimental outcome. It is not uncommon to do experimentation and find a third explanation for casework, i.e. police say one thing, the suspect says another, and the bloodstains suggest a third explanation. Whatever the results, records should be kept and hopefully shared with other investigators for future understanding of bloodstain pattern physical evidence.

CONCLUSIONS

Blood dynamics, as Dr Paul Kirk named this scientific discipline, is varied and complex. For economic as well as academic reasons, a large body of information must be assimilated from diverse science research and reapplied as forensic science data. The present publication is an attempt to expand the information sources presently available in this discipline. It is not and cannot be exhaustive because applicable studies are ongoing. It is hoped that students of different viewpoints and technical background will find something useful which will lead to a desire for more information. Specialization is necessary in our growing technological world. The availability of science specialties providing research in such fields as rheology and non-Newtonian fluid mechanics can compensate for the lack of funds in forensic science research. There is much knowledge still to be discovered which will continue the legacy of Dr Paul Kirk.

REFERENCES

1.   Kirk, Paul (1968) *The Credibility of Physical Evidence Testimony.* Presentation notes for Criminal Law Seminar 15 December 1968 in the Paul Kirk Papers. UC Bancroft Library Archives. Berkeley.

2.   MacDonell, Herbert Leon and Brooks, Brian A. (1977) 'Detection and significance of blood in firearms', in *Legal Medical Annual* (Ed. Cyril H. Wecht). Appleton-Crofts, New York, pp. 187–199.

3.   Bevel, Tom and Gardner, Ross M. (1997) *Bloodstain Pattern Analysis with an Introduction to Crime Scene Reconstruction.* CRC, Boca Raton, FL, p. 62.

4.   Ibid, p. 61.

5.   *Blood in Slow Motion* (1991) Video. Home Office Main Laboratory, London.

BIBLIOGRAPHY

Albert, Solomon N. (1971) *Blood Volume and Extracellular Fluid Volume* (2nd edn). Charles C. Thomas, Springfield, IL.

Allen, Robert W., Kahn, Richard A. and Baldassare, Joseph J. (1986) 'Advances in the production of blood cell substitutes with alternative technologies', in *New Frontiers in Blood Banking* (eds C.H. Wallas and L.J. McCarthy). American Association of Blood Banks, Washington, DC.

Balthazard, V., Piedelievre, R., Desoille, H. and DeRobert, L. (1939) *Etude des gouttes de sang projecte*. Presented at the 22nd Congress of Forensic Medicine, Paris, France.

Bevel, Tom and Gardner, Ross M. (1997) *Bloodstain Pattern Analysis with an Introduction to Crime Scene Reconstruction*. CRC, Boca Raton, FL.

Blood in Slow Motion (1993) Video. Home Office (Formerly Metropolitan Police Laboratory) Main Laboratory, London.

Bockchoon, Pak, Young, I. Cho and Choi, Steven U.S. (1990) 'Separation and reattachment of nonNewtonian fluid flows in sudden expansion pipe', *Journal of Non-Newtonian Fluid Mechanics*, **37**(5), 175–199.

Boger, D.V. and Walters, K. (1993) *Rheological Series 4, Rheological Phenomena in Focus*. Elsevier, Amsterdam.

Bürkholz, Armin (1989) *Droplet Separation*. Verlagsgesellschaft, Republic of Germany.

Chisum, J. (1998) *Pitfalls in Bloodstain Pattern Interpretation*. California Association of Criminalists Spring Meeting, Monterey.

Chmiel, Horst and Walitza, Eckehard (1980) *On the Rheology of Blood and Synovial Fluids*. John Wiley and Sons, London.

Concise Encyclopedia of Science and Technology (4th edn) (1998) (Ed. Sybil P. Parker). McGraw-Hill, NY, p. 907.

Dailey, John F. (1998) *Blood*. Medical Consulting Group, Arlington, Massachusetts.

Dictionary of Physics (1977) (Ed. Valerie Illingworth). Penguin Group, London.

DiMaio, Vincent J.M. (1999) *Gunshot Wounds Practical Aspects of Firearms, Ballistics, and Forensic Techniques* (2nd edn). CRC, Boca Raton, FL.

Franklin-Barbajosa, Cassandra (May 1992) 'DNA profiling. The new science of identity', *National Geographic* **181**(5), 112.

Geddes, L.A. (1970) *The Direct and Indirect Measurement of Blood Pressure*. Year Book Medical Publishers, Chicago.

Harris, Henry (1932) *California's Medical Story*. J.W. Stacey, San Francisco.

Heaton, Wm, Andrew L. (1986) 'Enhancement of cellular elements in new frontiers in blood banking', in *New Frontiers in Blood Banking*. AABB, Washington DC.

Hein, Morris, Best, Leo R., Pattison, Scott and Arena, Susan (1993) *College Chemistry an Introduction to General, Organic, and Biochemistry* (5th edn). Brooks/Cole, Pacific Grove, CA.

Houck, Max M. (2000) 'What is color? How is it perceived?', in *Color Analysis in Forensic Science Workshop*. AAFS 52nd Annual Meeting, Reno, Nevada.

James, Stuart H. and Eckert, William (1989) *Interpretation of Bloodstain Evidence at Crime Scenes.* Elsevier, Amsterdam, p. 52.

Janson, H.W. (1964) *History of Art.* Prentice-Hall, New Jersey, and Harry N. Abrams, New York.

Kirk, Paul L. (1962) *The Expert Witness in Criminal Cases.* Summary of the Proceedings of the 40th Annual Conference National Legal Aid and Defender Association, San Francisco.

Kirk, Paul L. (1963) *Necessary Expert Witnesses in Criminal Matters.* Paul Kirk Papers, Bancroft Library, University of California, Berkeley.

Kirk, Paul L. (1967) *Blood – a Neglected Criminalistics Research Area, Law Enforcement. Science and Technology.* (Ed. S.A. Yefsky). Academic Press, London.

Kirk, Paul L. (1968) *Blood Spot Analysis.* Presentation Notes Lecture at 4th Annual Criminal Law Seminar, San Francisco. Paul Kirk Papers, UC Bancroft Library, Berkeley

Kirk, Paul L. (1974) *Blood: Physical Investigation, in Crime Investigation* (2nd edn). (Ed. John I. Thornton). John Wiley and Sons, Philadelphia, p. 172.

Laber, Terry (1986) 'Diameter of a bloodstain as a function of origin, distance fallen, and volume of drop', *IABPA News* **12**(1), 12–16.

Laber, Terry and Epstein, Barton P. (1983) *Experiments and Practical Exercises in Bloodstain Pattern Analysis.* Callan Publishing, Minneapolis, Minnesota.

Lee, Henry C., Gaenxslen, R.E. and Pagliaro, Elaine M. (1986) 'Blood volume estimation', *International Association of Bloodstain Pattern Analysts News* **3**(2), 47–55.

MacDonell, Herbert Leon and Bialousz, Lorraine Fiske (1971) *Flight Characteristic and Stain Patterns of Human Blood.* US Government, Washington DC.

MacDonell, Herbert Leon (1983) *Bloodstain Pattern Interpretation.* Laboratory of Forensic Science, Corning, NY.

MacDonell, Herbert Leon (1991) Inquiry held under section 475 of the Crimes Act 1900 into the conviction of Alexander Lindsay (formerly Alexander McLeod-Lindsay), 28 May, p. 941. Australia Federal Court. Sydney, Australia. Decided July 1991.

Mandel, Emanuel E. (1966) 'Laboratory diagnosis of hemorrhagic disorders', in *Todd-Sanford Clinical Diagnoses by Laboratory Methods* (Eds Israel Davidsohn and Benjamin Wells). W.B. Saunders, Philadelphia.

Moss, Donald W., Henderson, A. Ralph and Kachmar, John F. (1986) *Textbook of Clinical Chemistry* (Ed. Norbert W. Tietz). W.B. Saunders, Philadelphia.

Nelson, Douglas A. and Morris, Michael W. (1991) 'Basic examination of blood', in *Clinical Diagnosis and Management by Laboratory Methods* (18th edn) (Ed. John Bernard Henry). W.B. Saunders, Philadelphia.

Nelson, Douglas A. and Rodak, Bernadette F. (1983) 'Hematology', in *Clinical Guide to Laboratory Tests* (Ed. Norbert W. Tietz). W.B. Saunders, Philadelphia.

Nubar, Yves (1966) *The Laminar Flow of a Composite Fluid an Approach to the Rheology of Blood.* New York Academy of Sciences, NY.

Piotrowski, Eduard (1895) *Ueber Entstehung, Form, Richtung u. Ausbreitung der Blutduren nach Hiebwunden des Kopfes.* Golos Printing, Elmira, NY, 1992.

Pizzola, P.A., Roth, Steven, and DeForest, Peter (1986) 'Blood droplet dynamics – I and II', *Journal of Forensic Sciences* **31**(1), 36–64.

Raymond, Anthony, Smith, E.R., and Liesegang, J. (1996) 'Oscillating blood droplets – implications for crime scene reconstruction', *Science and Justice* **36**(3), 161–171.

Sadhal, S.S., Ayyaswamy, P. S, and Chung, J. N. (1997) *Transport Phenomena with Drops and Bubbles.* Springer, New York.

Saferstein, Richard (1990) *Criminalistics: An Introduction to Forensic Science* (4th edn). Prentice Hall, Englewood Cliffs, New Jersey.

Sears, Francis Weston and Zemansky, Mark W. (1961) *University Physics Complete Edition*, Addison-Wesley Publishing, Reading, Massachusetts.

Selby, M.J. (1985) *The Earth's Changing Surface, an Introduction to Geomorphology.* Clarendon Press, Oxford.

Sohmer, Paul R. (1979) 'The pathophysiology of hemorrhagic shock', in *Hemotherapy in Trauma and Surgery.* AABB, Washington DC.

Tietz, Norbert W. (Ed.) (1983) *Clinical Guide to Laboratory Tests.* W.B. Saunders, Philadelphia.

Tanner, R.I. and Walters, Kenneth (1998) *Rheology: An Historical Perspective,* Elsevier, Amsterdam.

Tullis, James L. (1976) *Clot.* Charles C. Thomas, Springfield, IL.

Vennard, John K., and Street, Robert L. (1982) *Elementary Fluid Mechanics* (6th edn). John Wiley and Sons, New York.

Wambaugh, Joseph (1989) *The Blooding.* William Morrow, NY.

Walters, Kenneth (1975) *Rheometry.* Chapman and Hall, London.

White, Harvey E. (1962) *Modern College Physics* (4th edn). D. Van Nostrand, Princeton, NJ.

Whitmore, R.L. (1968) *Rheology of the Circulation.* Pergamon Press, Oxford.

Whorlow, R.W. (1992) *Rheological Techniques* (2nd edn). Ellis Horwood, New York.

Wonder, Anita Y. (1994) *An Objective Approach to the Identification of Gunshot Impact Spatter Patterns.* American Academy of Forensic Sciences Annual Meeting, San Antonio, Texas.

AUTHOR INDEX